Cultureship

The **A C B**s

of **Business Leadership**

Jason E. Bingham

RIVER GROVE
BOOKS

Published by River Grove Books
Austin, TX
www.greenleafbookgroup.com

Distributed by River Grove Books

For ordering information or special discounts for bulk purchases, please contact River Grove Books at PO Box 91869, Austin, TX, 78709, 512.891.6100.

Design and composition by Greenleaf Book Group LLC
Cover design by Greenleaf Book Group LLC
Cover image: © Elnur, 2012. Used under license from Shutterstock.com.

Publisher's Cataloging-In-Publication Data
(Prepared by The Donohue Group, Inc.)
Bingham, Jason E.
   Cultureship : the ACBs of business leadership / Jason E. Bingham.—1st ed.
   p. ; cm.
   Issued also as an ebook.
   ISBN: 978-1-938416-21-7 (hdbd.)
   ISBN: 978-1-938416-18-7 (pbk.)
   1. Corporate culture. 2. Management. 3. Leadership. I. Title.
HD58.7 .B56 2013
302.35   2012953714

Print ISBN: 978-1-938416-18-7
eBook ISBN: 978-1-934816-19-4

12 13 14 15 10 9 8 7 6 5 4 3 2 1
First Edition

*To the many mentors who have guided me throughout
my life, especially my wife Shelby and
my three kids, Alex, Sara Catherine, and Bailey.*

*You teach me something with every precious
moment I spend with each of you.*

Contents

Preface vii

Acknowledgments...xi

To the Reader..xiii

Chapter 1 Belief: Integrity Leads to Profit 1

Chapter 2 Belief: Trusting Others Expands Profit 17

Chapter 3 Belief: Associates Own the Culture 29

Chapter 4 Belief: Leaders Don't Direct, They Lead 43

Chapter 5 Belief: Everyone Wants to Grow, Serve,
               and Perform 63

Chapter 6 Belief: Enlightened Teams Achieve Superhuman
               Success 85

Chapter 7 Belief: Purposeful Associates Create Loyal Customers
               Who Maximize Business Results (the ACBs) 97

Chapter 8 Belief: Excellence Is Driven from the Ground Up...........109

Chapter 9 Belief: Changing Culture Can Change Results
               Quickly..129

Chapter 10 Belief: Strong Leaders Follow Culture 143

Chapter 11 Results Are the Real Starting Point 171

Appendix 189

Index 209

About the Author 219

Preface

My professional-life experiences have taught me that culture is directly connected to profit and that the way to deliver that culture can be taught and learned. The few leaders who have seen (or, more accurately, *felt*) high-performing cultures know this to be true. There are even fewer leaders who understand how to build these cultures to successfully deliver substantial business results. This book is the synthesis of my professional-life experiences, and my way of paying forward the blessing of seeing, feeling, and building high-performance cultures.

This culture wizardry is not an inherent talent I was born with. In fact, I am a short, scrawny guy with few talents. Over time and through trial and error, I developed the ability to lead cultural transformation and bring about great profitability. And you can too.

As a novice leader thrown into an experienced business world, I immediately started devouring books on leadership. My wife, Shelby, thought I was nuts because everything I read seemed to be slightly different versions of the same thing. Although I learned something from each of these books, overall they were lacking in meaningful content. They could never replace real-life experiences. They also did not bring together the total picture.

After being placed in a strong-culture environment, I finally realized that developing high-performing cultures could be taught and learned. After some practice, I learned how to build high-performing cultures. Incredible success followed directly from those lessons.

It was extremely fortunate: just about every career experience I had provided another lesson needed to become a great leader. As I integrated the lessons into each subsequent phase of my career and refined them, a system began to emerge. This is the system that shapes my leadership behaviors. I wrote this book to pass this system—what I call *cultureship*—along to others to help them improve their professional lives. Contrary to popular belief, leadership is not the answer to every business problem. Strong leaders follow culture.

Things happen for a reason. Call it karma. Call it God's will. Call it serendipity. But don't call it luck. No matter your beliefs, each of us is here for a reason. We are here to make a difference, to serve a purpose. The experiences in each of our lives build our capabilities to serve that purpose. In other words, our experiences fulfill life's purpose. For me, that purpose is building strong-culture leadership.

Once you understand these beliefs and how they fit together as a unified whole, you will be on your way to becoming a great leader. You will feel the thrill of helping associates find the power within them that everyone has. You will see the inspiring success that comes when you put enlightened teams together. And you will enjoy the business results you reap when your high-performing culture comes to life.

Cultureship is practical. It is not some way-out concept that takes a lifetime to figure out. Yes, I had to practice and screw up and then get it right and then screw it up again, and so on and so on. Yet through those experiences, I learned how to be a culture leader. My gift to you is a practical and condensed version of that process so that you too may become a culture leader who delivers premier business results.

The real beauty is that you can integrate cultureship into every realm of your life. As you put these practical beliefs and tools into action, you become a culture leader. As you become a culture leader within your work world, you immediately recognize that cultureship is a total life system, not just a business system. You can bring cultureship home. You can bring cultureship to church and your community—even to your soccer team. You can make a real difference for others. You will see that it is possible to make a difference for the greater community—and maybe even the world—through this system.

Acknowledgments

The business leaders of my career are the teachers of Cultureship. Jeff Watson was the foremost of these leaders for me. He learned much of his Cultureship lessons from Jess Newbern, who built the amazing culture in the Roanoke office of Trane. Without these two gentlemen, this book would not exist. Other key leaders who shaped Cultureship for me include Matte Anderson, Felix Wilson, Donny Simmons, Dave Regnery, and my dad. These people as well as other leaders in my community and church and authors of leadership books are due a large thank you for their contribution to Cultureship. From Sherman the shoeshine guy to my mom and dad, thank you!

To the Reader

The book is arranged to help you learn the subject and immediately apply the lessons through practical tools. You will read about a real-life story within one of my careers, which will end with a belief I learned during this time. Then, you will read more conceptual information and data that explains the belief. Finally, each chapter will end with a business tool you can use to build that belief within your team or organization. In the chapter that follows, we will continue with the next phase of my career. As you get toward the end of the book, you will learn how the beliefs I have learned throughout my career actually come together into a system of beliefs. It is this system of beliefs that forms the definition and execution of "Cultureship."

1

Belief: Integrity Leads to Profit

SERVING OTHERS WHEN YOU ARE ON
100 PERCENT COMMISSION!

Holy cow! There I was, in Birmingham, Alabama, with my new wife, Shelby, and we were moving into our second apartment. Our first apartment was in LaCrosse, Wisconsin. I had just accepted an offer from the only company I would ever work for (at least to this point), Trane. Trane sends their newly hired sales engineers to LaCrosse for six months of training, which corresponded with our first six months of marriage. It was way too much fun, yet for southerners, it was also way too much snow!

When we moved into our second apartment as a married couple in Birmingham, I started the real job. With my rose-colored glasses well attached to my face, I jumped in with my usual level of energy—picture a Jack Russell terrier after you throw a tennis ball. They started me off with the "shit" accounts. In other words, as the new sales guy, I got the accounts that no one else wanted. Yet, those accounts were tennis balls

I was excited to chase, and I soon made some small wins by making the very small accounts worth a little more. I had to. The compensation was 100 percent commission. If I didn't sell, we didn't eat.

While I was growing up, my mom taught me that if I focused on serving others, the rest would fall in to place. I was not conscious of it at the time, but that is exactly what I did at Trane from the get-go. I served passionately, responded quickly, and did my best to do the right thing. Yet, the rose-colored glasses began to fall off at times.

My small successes were being overshadowed with many, many mistakes. I ordered the wrong voltage for an air conditioner and had to pay to get it right. I ordered the wrong thermostats and had to pay to get them right. I made a commitment to my customer that I could not keep or was not possible and, you guessed it, had to pay to get it right. And in Trane, when one guy makes a mistake, others pay for it, too. The 100 percent commission means that every salesperson who helps sell the job gets a piece of the pie. It also means that the same salespeople share every mistake. In my desire to serve, I was tripping over my inability to get it right.

These cost blunders drew concern from my peers, as did my low commission rate. Low income because of lower commission rates and high outcome because of all the extra expenses from mistakes was not the best business model for them. It was not the best personal business model either. Although I was on a "draw" that ensured a consistent monthly check, it was not a free draw. Essentially I was going deeper and deeper and deeper in debt. In fact, after two years on the job I was in my deepest hole yet with a debt of over $50,000. The pressure was building from everywhere—my peers, my boss, my wife, and maybe most of all, myself. I was frustrated and terrified of failure.

As I look back, the moment of truth was a health-care project with my newest customer. Seeing the need to get me more business, my boss moved some accounts around and gave me a large mechanical-engineering firm. Mechanical-engineering firms actually design the HVAC systems in buildings. Again, I jumped right in with speedy service. The lead designer, Kevin, and I hit it off immediately. He liked the attention and response. He felt he could trust me because I was always upfront and honest with him. He would design his jobs around Trane equipment when, in the past, he had preferred our competition. I was moving ahead, yet the large deficit in my draw account was weighing on me.

Kevin called one weekend and told me that he had a major hospital project that had to be designed by Monday morning. It was going to bid within two weeks, and then the building would be fast-tracked so that it would be completed before the summer months. Mechanical engineers like Kevin draw up the plans for HVAC systems, and they also create the specifications for those HVAC pieces. The stricter the requirements, the fewer the vendors able to comply. It is even possible to have a specification so strict that only one vendor can comply.

"Could you help me make the selections and lay out the system?" Kevin asked. I, of course, said yes. I met him for lunch on Saturday. He was clear: "Your equipment should be the preference, yet not exclusive." I told him, "I got it, no problem," and headed home to get it done. As I was digging into the selections, two words seemed to rise from the page: "high efficiency." I knew Trane had a huge efficiency advantage over our competitors, and I could lock out the competition if I selected and specified the right units.

My heart started beating faster, and I began to sweat. I was considering doing what it took to make commission, rather than doing the right thing for my customer. If I chose to write the specification around a proprietary efficiency, I would receive a very high commission. Since

Kevin was constrained by time, he would most likely send it through to the final document without noticing that I had limited competition. It would be easy to make a quick buck, yet it would be abusing the trust he had given me. I would be risking the long-term relationship with a valued customer and my reputation as a salesperson.

I remember standing up and going to the kitchen. My mind started talking to itself. *You sure have worked hard for this customer. You deserve to be paid for your efforts.* Picture that little red devil dude with a pitchfork on my shoulder. Just as I was about to walk out of the kitchen, the door swung open and hit me right in the head. It was my wife, yet it was also God. His message was pretty darn clear: "Do not do it, dummy."

And I didn't. I wrote the specification so that it required high efficiency yet also allowed for multiple competitors. I even looked up my competitors' catalogs to make sure they could bid the project. That decision put me on the right long-term path. As it turned out, Kevin mentioned that project some time later as he and I were drinking a beer. He said, "I assumed you would lock that spec down, so I double checked. You made sure others could bid, didn't you?"

"Yes, I did."

"Knowing I can trust you is a big deal, Jason. Thanks," he said.

It took me a while to get off draw, yet looking back it was so clear. There finally came a time when I no longer had to follow up with my customers on projects. They would call me and ask if I wanted to work with them on a job. There was also a time when my customers began wanting me to make money. They would make suggestions such as, "This one is not a tight job, so price it fair, yet not cheap." Soon, I had a huge share of their business at a much higher commission rate.

The value I added to their businesses by focusing on their best interests had changed me from a vendor into a partner. They needed me. I reduced their risk and increased the value they added to their customers. The trust I built turned the process of price negotiation into a time for discussing the best way to stay on budget. We were making a profit together.

Shortcuts often don't save you any time at all. It's important to do the right thing and get things done right. When you do the right thing for long enough, the results come. The results came in wonderful ways for me, which culminated in receiving the Eagle award for the first salesperson to exceed quota in the first five years of his or her career.

LIVING WITH INTEGRITY LEADS TO SUCCESS

Life has many choices, and the choices you make determine the quality of your life. Integrity is aligning your choices with your values. The actions of people with high integrity match their words, and their feet match their thoughts. Integrity is what happens when no one is looking. With integrity, you make choices that serve the greater good, and your decisions are the best you can find. Without integrity, you will tend to make choices that are more self-centered. If you are focused on your own benefit, you will make decisions that are useful and profitable to you without considering the impact those decisions may have on others. Using sales as an example, when you are on 100 percent commission or have some similar compensation system, every time you sell something you earn a portion of the net profit of that sale. This can create a habit of thinking short term about personal profit. You can make decisions without integrity to get the short-term profit. Being self-centered can mean making more money—in the short term.

On the other hand, you can make decisions that match your conscience. You can recognize that the situation affects all involved and then do your best to make the right decision. This might mean not selling a product or a service because it is not the right thing for the customer or because you know there is a better option available. Though it may seem paradoxical, deciding to not sell because your competitor has a better option probably is the right decision.

If you take a moment to closely consider all of the impacts of your decisions, you will find that integrity leads to profit. You might "get away" with selling something that is not right for a customer initially. You might even make a quick buck doing it. Yet, it's unlikely you'll be able to sell to that same customer again. The truth is rarely hidden for long. In my simple sales example, the end user of the product will most likely find out that he actually had better options or that he made a poor choice. He might hear from someone else that he made a mistake. And when that end user attributes that mistake to working with you, you will pay the price.

Unhappy customers talk about their experiences, and one disgruntled customer can influence many people. If you consistently serve yourself rather than the best interests of your customers, that one customer will become many. At a minimum, people who hear from these disgruntled customers will be wary when dealing with you. They may ask more questions than usual or do more behind-the-scenes investigation or get more quotes from other vendors, and all those actions would cost you time and money. You would have to answer more questions. You would have to battle more competitors. You would eventually decrease your market share, and more of your business would have to be priced competitively, which would reduce your company's profit. When you lose trust, you lose profit.

KEEP THE TRUTH OF THE MOMENT

Now, I want to spend some time talking about how to hold yourself to a higher level of integrity. I am not going to discuss the simple stuff. Either you are committed to doing the right thing or you are not. For the purposes of this discussion, I am going to assume that you are generally honest and have a desire to make the right choices after considering the needs of all involved.

You generally follow your conscience when you make choices. Your conscience is a set of beliefs you live by, and they can come from any of the experiences in your life. The problem is that you can be your biggest obstacle to integrity because your brain can build false beliefs. These false beliefs usually result in making poor choices, thus acting without integrity. For example, if you were to see a minor incident between two people, within seconds your brain would create some assumptions about the people involved. These assumptions may or may not be right, yet they could influence what you choose to see in the future and even your future decisions. Eventually, your brain can build false beliefs based on false assumptions.

For example, if my CFO were to ask a lot of questions about my decisions or direction, I might think she was challenging me, and my brain might start to think that she was out to get me, even though I may have very little information on which to base that assumption.

If in our next meeting I announce my vision and direction for our company and she asks, "Can you give us the data that led us to your decision to take us in that direction?" I might think she is trying to prove me wrong in front of the entire company. At this point, my assumptions would affect my decisions. I would probably send her less information in the future because I would be fearful about what she would do with it. My behavior would change based on the assumptions my brain made.

From the CFO's perspective, my behavior change would be palpable. She would no longer get the monthly reports and communication she used to get. She would start to wonder why I was holding back information, whether I no longer trusted her, and whether I was out to get her. With her thoughts and assumptions, she would start to treat me differently, which would only confirm my belief that she was out to get me.

I refer to this as a fictional story, but it was actually based on a series of events I witnessed. What is most interesting is that I know for a fact that the CFO actually thought the CEO was a great leader. She asked more questions so that she could help him support his direction with more facts. She was confident in his direction; he was just not communicating it well.

The point you should take away from this illustration is that our beliefs tend to prove themselves. When we form assumptions and beliefs, we tend to find the experiences and information that confirm our beliefs. Unfortunately, we also tend to ignore those experiences that are contradictory to our beliefs. In other words, we tend to find what we are looking for. Henry David Thoreau said it best: "There is no rule more invariable than that we are paid for our suspicions by finding what we suspect."

Integrity maxim #1: Never assume anything about anybody.

If you view someone through the glasses of your experiences alone, you risk losing the truth of the moment. Your brain tends to form beliefs on limited information, and those beliefs influence your decisions and changes in behavior toward that person. The person will pick up on your changed behavior and eventually change his or her own behavior accordingly. Instead of following our conscience, we follow our brain, which has some false assumptions and beliefs. To hold ourselves to the highest integrity, we need to constantly test all assumptions by talking directly to the people involved, rather than making up our own version of the story. We need to test our assumptions thoroughly before allowing them to become beliefs. Later in this chapter, you will read about a tool called "Direct with Respect," which has helped me control my brain's ability to create false assumptions and has improved my ability to act with utmost integrity.

Sherman's Simple Truth

The story in the last section reminds me of a shoeshine guy I was blessed to meet in the Chicago O'Hare International Airport. I didn't have much time, but I thought I could manage to squeeze in a quick shoeshine without a problem. Unfortunately, the line took longer than I thought. When I finally sat down in the high chair that allows clients getting their shoes shined to see over the heads of all the passersby (and thus makes the client feel somewhat like a king), my boarding time was within five minutes. Yes, I was feeling a little stressed.

Sherman, the shoeshine guy, looked like he was in his sixties, yet he had the energy of a thirty-year-old. He had a big smile. He asked me how much time I had, and I grimaced. He asked if he should do the quick version, and I said no. He said, "Okay, you will get my best shine and still be on time." I relaxed immediately as he went to work shining my shoes like it was the most important thing he could be doing.

He chatted with the young shoeshine guy next to him about a customer two weeks ago who ended up not having enough cash and asked if it would be okay to catch him later. Sherman told the customer no problem. One week later, that same customer came by and not only paid for the shine but also tipped Sherman an extra $100. The young guy said, "You are so lucky. Didn't you also have a reporter come by and write an article about you? How do you do it?"

Sherman lifted his head, for some reason looked me in the eyes, and said, "I figured out that if I don't let my head get in the way and just focus on passionately serving others, amazing things happen." For me, it was like a message from God, yet he was using Sherman, who was looking me right in the eye, to deliver it.

Sherman hit the nail on the head. I realized that if I could keep my head out of the way, it would probably be fairly easy for me to determine the right thing to do by looking for the reality of the situation. Then I would do the right thing. Then the right things would happen for me.

Sherman also pointed out that I should surround myself with people who don't let their head get in the way. I should pick leaders based on their integrity as much as their talent. This concept would serve me well as I moved into management.

ALL MINE AND NO ONE ELSE'S

My tendency to justify my past decisions or blame poor decisions on other people or events affects my ability to act with integrity. It might have its roots in the "fight or flight" instincts we have from the saber-toothed tiger days. When I make a bad decision or have a bad result, either my "fight" instinct can pop out to blame someone else, or my "flight" instinct will activate to justify my decision, rather than face the real consequences.

There are many legitimate reasons to blame or justify. In my world of HVAC at Trane, if it were sixty degrees all year long, our sales would be low and I could easily blame the weather for the poor business results. I could justify to my bosses that I really didn't have any options because the weather did not allow for a different result. And I would be right with my blame and justification.

But here's the problem with blaming and justifying. If the next year the weather is also sixty degrees all year long, I am going to have the same results. Since I did nothing different to address the situation, I learned nothing. The blame and justification will have reduced my ability to do the right thing because I am not learning from the experiences of my life. They also reduce my results because I am dependent on someone or something external to succeed. How can you succeed without learning from your past? How can you act with integrity when you continue to make the same wrong decisions? Isn't it just as wrong not to act when you should, as it is to do the wrong thing?

I like to use ARC International's "100%–0%" approach to life, which says I am 100 percent responsible for any result I touch and no one else has any responsibility. The key word here is "approach." Reality is clear. There are other people and issues that have some responsibility for the results I get. Yet we are not talking about reality. We are talking about approach. The best way to approach any situation is as if it is all mine and no one else's.

The approach works best because it is the best way to learn the lessons from any situation and make better decisions in the future. When I take full responsibility, I can be honest with myself on what I did well and what I could have done differently. I can even be creative on how I could have done it completely different for a better result. I do not spend any energy blaming others. Instead, I spend all my energy solving the problem and learning the lessons within the results.

**Integrity Maxim #2: Never give away any
authority for your results.**

Taking full responsibility for our results is more than just about compensation or business results. It is about our behavior and reputations. If I blame or justify the results I get, I am essentially giving other people or events the responsibility for *my* results. Think about that for a minute—once I blame others, I give them authority over my results. I am allowing others to decide my success. On the other hand, if I take a 100%–0% approach, I am taking full authority for my own results. This is a *much* more empowering approach to life and an important way to act with integrity.

THE FRONTLINE PEOPLE MUST ALWAYS DO RIGHT

One final thought before we leave this phase in my career and the lessons it gave me: during this time, I learned the importance of personal integrity. Yet, I also learned how important it was for my peers, my boss, and my direct reports. In fact, I learned that I needed to surround myself with people who held this same belief if I were to be successful.

As I moved into management, this meant that I needed to hire based on values and integrity. I needed to develop, coach, and mentor my team with a focus on integrity. I also needed to promote and fire based on integrity. When I realized the importance of integrity, it set up my strong belief that high-performance teams can only be possible if they are built on a foundation of integrity. I was ready to start building that high-performance team.

TOOLS

Direct with Respect

To make sure we do not create false assumptions or beliefs, we need a tool that allows for introspection and candor. The direct with respect (DWR) tool will help you build trust and teamwork in your organization by having people discuss issues together and then hold each other accountable to the guiding principles of the organization. The tool helps deliver the total picture of reality, versus the small picture of information that you actually experience.

The DWR approach says,

- I am going to tell you what is on my mind (direct).
- I am going to try to tell it to you in the moment (direct).
- I may mess up my communication, but at least I will put it on the table (direct).
- My only intent is to help you, me, and us (respect).
- I am sure I am at least partially wrong with my perception (respect).
- I need to hear your thoughts to get it right (respect).

How to Use DWR

The DWR tool is relatively straightforward, but it takes courage to start the discussion. There are four steps to using the DWR tool:

1. **Share your intent.** "My goal is to help you, me, and us by telling you exactly what is on my mind, while listening to your thoughts, because my perceptions are not completely right."

2. **Speak what is on your mind.** Use the following rules to be specific, yet concise. Tell the other person when, where, what, and how:

- When it happened (e.g., last Friday)
- Where it happened (e.g., during our team meeting)
- What behavior happened (e.g., you closed your eyes)
- How it impacted you (e.g., it made me feel like you didn't care about the team)

3. **Hear their thoughts.** Now that you have concisely communicated your concern, ask for their thoughts. Listen openly and search for understanding. Ask clarifying questions.

4. **Collaborate to find a joint solution.** Stay away from blame or justification. Instead, look for future-oriented solutions, next steps, and expectations.

Practice using the DWR tool in your office often. You will find that associates naturally adapt to this approach and even start using the term "direct with respect" commonly. When this happens, your culture starts to move toward high-performance teamwork.

100%–0%

As described earlier, the 100%–0% tool is an approach to life that takes full responsibility for all results, while placing zero responsibility on anyone else. It is an approach, not a reality. The best way to make this approach systemic within your team or organization is to set the mantra that there will be no excuses and no blame. Make it fun to catch someone in the organization blaming something or making an excuse. When "no excuses" becomes cultural, every associate feels very comfortable calling out excuses and blame when they happen and every associate also feels comfortable admitting to their excuses and/or blame (we all go there).

Most important, if you can create a culture where excuses are not acceptable answers, the only alternative will be to solve the problem.

Everyone will be held accountable to a higher level of integrity and also to finding solutions to their problems.

Making no excuses cultural is actually relatively easy, and it can take hold quickly. It takes five steps:

1. Read the 100%–0% article, "Results versus Reasons and Stories or 100% Responsibility," which I found from ARC International, Ltd., in Columbus, Ohio.

2. Have the leadership team read the article and discuss at their next leadership meeting. Suggest that "no excuses" is now a mantra of your culture. Ask to add it to your guiding principles.

3. Ask each leader to facilitate the same discussion within their teams.

4. One month later, create posters that say "100%–0%, No Excuses, We Own Our Performance" or something like that.

5. In the next meeting, catch people making excuses or passing blame. Do it in a lighthearted way, calling it out yet admitting that you all do it. Continue to call it out in a fun way until you see others do the same, and praise them.

Then just sit back and watch this approach take off. I have personally seen it work wonders very quickly in many different organizations and teams.

2

Belief: Trusting Others Expands Profit

YOU CAN'T LEAD WHEN YOU ARE ALL ALONE

Here we go again. At this point, Shelby and I had moved from Knoxville, Tennessee, to LaCrosse, Wisconsin, and then to Birmingham, Alabama. With the retirement of a forty-five-year veteran salesperson, my boss asked me to relocate to Huntsville, Alabama, to fill the vacancy. With our first child, Alex, too young to argue, we decided to head to northern Alabama. As it turned out, Huntsville was much more "southern" than Birmingham, and we loved it.

Starting over was refreshing. I was able to leave behind all the mistakes I had made in my first five years at Trane and start fresh with new customers. It was a lot of work building relationships with a substantial customer base, yet I had more confidence and experience with what to do and how to do it. I also knew that I was working with integrity. After two years in Huntsville, I had formed solid relationships with a broad customer base, and the work got much easier.

As I got closer to my customers, I recognized that they had new needs. Building automation (computerized "thermostats" in big buildings that can be operated remotely for scheduling and easy coordination for optimal energy usage) was a major need and a major problem. Contractors told me the building-automation subcontractors were a pain to work with. Building owners told me the systems installed were inadequate and service of those systems was unavailable. Trane had a building-automation system, yet we were falling into the same inadequacy trap.

I sold these systems and, again, screwed up a lot. I sometimes sold the wrong system or I didn't communicate clearly to the installers which system I had sold. But another part of the problem was that the building-automation experts were in Birmingham, and there was no local talent. So I called my boss and asked if I could build my own building-automation team. He agreed, and I started recruiting internal talent and hiring others from outside the company. We also started partnerships with local installers to do some of the heavy lifting.

This is where it got really interesting. I had a full-time job as a sales engineer with a large-equipment sales quota, yet I was also running a small building-automation team and served as the main estimator of these systems. At one point I had two phones and a walkie-talkie on my belt. Pick your word—bananas, hectic, crazy, ballistic. It was all of these and more.

From the get-go, I realized that I could not manage my team and my installers and do all the necessary estimates while also trying to fulfill the duties of my full-time job. My drive to serve others was building a one-man show that would bring us all down. My out-of-control workload was also damaging my young family. Shelby was tired of me leaving early and coming home late. I tried to fix this by getting up even earlier so I could come home earlier, but I missed the 6 p.m. deadline more often than I made it.

One Thursday morning I awoke at 3:00 a.m. and left for work soon thereafter. I needed to get a bunch of estimates done and prepare for an 8:00 a.m. meeting about a major equipment sale. I had completed the estimates and started working on the big project when one of my phones beeped. It was our largest building-automation customer, Huntsville Hospital, calling about a major issue they had in their OR wing. They needed immediate service as well as an immediate proposal to fix the problem for good. After hanging up with the hospital's maintenance supervisor, I promptly freaked out. There was no way I could be prepared for my big project meeting and serve my biggest building-automation customer at the same time. I had to make a choice.

Just as I was pulling out my second handful of hair, two angels walked into the room. One was Eddie, our best installer partner. The other was Bobby, our best technician. They had just eaten breakfast and were ready to start work for the day. As they walked in with coffee in hand, they could tell (probably from the hair all over my desk) that something wasn't right. I was close with these guys, so I dumped my bucket.

Looking back, I was a complete idiot. In my mind there were two options—the major project or the major customer. Bobby and Eddie immediately realized the third option—they could help. Imagine that! I didn't have to do it all myself! I could trust my partners. And that is exactly what happened. Since they could not help with the major project, they immediately started working on the issue at Huntsville Hospital. They decided that Bobby would immediately go to the hospital to get the ORs up and running. He would then phone back to Eddie, who would work up the estimate for the long-term solution. They trashed their coffees and headed out the door.

I sometimes stop everything and try to take an objective look at what I am doing, and I'm often completely dismayed with how silly I can be. This was one of those times. The quick shift from hair pulling to problem solved was an awakening. It provided a visual and emotional image of what I was missing all along. If I could trust my partners, we could all get a whole lot more done together and have a whole lot more fun getting it done.

By lunch, my major project was sold, Huntsville Hospital's problem was solved, and the hospital had issued us a purchase order for the fix. Bobby, Eddie, and I had lunch, and then I took the rest of the day off. On the way home to spend much-needed time with my wife, my mind contrasted my current feelings of excitement and progress from the morning's feelings of being out of control. I decided to figure out how I could maintain the current feeling of excitement and stay away from the earlier negative feelings.

As my mind explored these questions, I looked back on the earlier years of my career. Although it took three years, once I built trust in my Birmingham teammates and customers, work got much easier. I didn't have to spend any time checking up on people or taking on more responsibilities that others could do. Once I gave my Huntsville partners and customers my trust, business got much easier there too. Now it was happening again. I was finally giving my trust to my building-automation team and life was getting fun.

LEADERS MUST TRUST AND CONSULT WITH FOLLOWERS

The first time I heard the phrase "those who don't trust are not trustworthy," I thought, *Horsepucky!* It didn't make any sense. It is certainly possible to not trust someone who has wronged you in the past while still maintaining your core values. I can think of relationships I have today in which my level of trust is skeptical at best, but I still behave in a trustworthy manner. Or do I? Now that I think of it, relationships in which I don't have full trust are the toughest to manage. Is it because I don't trust the other person, he or she doesn't trust me, or both?

If you don't trust an employee who works under you, you likely ask them more questions. You delegate less to them. You have fewer conversations with them. You are less likely to have social interactions with them. At company meetings, you probably avoid them. In meetings, you may challenge them or roll your eyes.

People know when they are being treated differently from their peers. And, as you learned in the last chapter, their minds take over and fill in the gaps with assumptions when communication is poor. Their minds assume that you don't like them or don't respect them or don't trust them or that you are out to get them. Any conclusion their mind makes will result in them treating you differently than they would if they did not *perceive* that you were treating them differently. Moreover, your inability to trust them has likely created the equal and opposite response—they don't trust you either. You are not trustworthy in their minds.

I learned early in my career that when I gave trust, things became very easy. Trusting others provided me with partners to help me get things done, and when I trusted others, it was also much easier to get things done. When trust was high with my "followers," the work got much simpler. I no longer had to follow up or ask more questions or over communicate. The work became more organic and flowed smoothly. Looking back, I learned that this state of flow expands profit.

Trust also leads to inclusion. When we trust someone, we want that person involved—especially if she has value to add to the process. When we include followers in the decision process, they contribute and feel useful. When they feel they contribute in reaching a decision, they are on board immediately, which makes it even easier to get things done.

THE SPEED OF TRUST

In his book *The Speed of Trust: The One Thing that Changes Everything*, Stephen Covey describes trust as the combination of character and competency. In other words, trust requires both integrity and your belief that something can happen. I think Covey is right on the money. It may be difficult to trust someone if you don't think that he acts with integrity. And it would be hard to trust someone to do a job if he has limited necessary experience or ability or is poorly organized.

There is another important distinction that needs to be made. There is a difference between trust and respect. As discussed, there are many reasons not to trust someone, but this does not mean that it is okay to treat a person without respect.

Now, there is no doubt that I treat people without respect. As you have already seen, I screw up all the time. My point is that I don't think it is the right thing to do. We don't know what the other person has gone through. We have not walked in their shoes. We all have our burdens to bear.

So here is the point. If we can identify the real reason for our lack of trust and discuss it directly with the person, while always treating that person with respect, we make trusting relationships the priority, which sends all the right messages about our intent as a leader. We have the courage to give our trust. It is amazing what people will do to honor the gift. A great first step to building strong, trusting relationships is to trust freely. In fact, I believe that the speed with which others get things done is in direct relationship to the amount of trust we place in them. When we place high trust in each other, there is very little overlap or redundancy in work. Things get done in the most efficient and effective way. Efficient and effective equals profitable. Trusting others expands profit.

When you trust associates in your company, you give them the authority to make decisions, spend money, and serve customers. In other words, you empower them. Researchers at Cornell University conducted a study (discussed in Daniel Pink's *Drive: The Surprising Truth about What Motivates Us*) to see if empowerment really had an impact on business. The researchers selected 160 companies that empowered employees and 160 companies with a top-down approach. The researchers then dug deep into the financials of these companies. They found that the empowering companies grew an average of four times the rate of the top-down companies! Yes, *four* times. Now *that* is expanded profit!

They also learned that the empowering companies had one-third the turnover of the top-down companies. As Frederick F. Reichheld discusses in his book *The Loyalty Effect: The Hidden Force Behind Growth, Profits, and Lasting Value*, it is the tenure of associates that also drives increases in profitability. In his detailed study, Reichheld confirmed that productivity of associates almost doubled by year five, and year five annual-profit contributions of associates was over ten times that of year one.

So leaders and companies that trust their associates dramatically expand profit by increasing the energy from each of their associates and by increasing the time the associates stay with the company. With more time, associates become more effective, which drives profit even further.

THE POWER OF TRUSTING PARTNERS

Eddie Shaver was my controls-wiring installer back in Huntsville during the time that we were having trouble with capacity. I was trying to do too much, and it was taking way too much time to do the controls-estimating process. Something had to give for us to grow the business and, fortunately, Eddie gave it. He put his trust in me.

Our estimating process was as follows. I would collect the plans that detailed the installation of the controls project. I would make a copy for Eddie and ask him to come pick it up. I would then estimate the equipment portion of the installation while waiting on Eddie to provide his estimate. Once I received Eddie's estimate there would inevitably be questions. What did you include? Do you have this? What did you exclude? Have I estimated all the equipment you need? The process was time consuming and slow.

One day, Eddie came to me with an idea. "Jason, what if I just trust you to estimate my installation portion?" he said. *What a crazy question*, I thought. He was going to trust me with his business? "I can tell you what it costs for each thermostat and for the big pieces of equipment. You can gauge from those costs the cost to do specialty items. If we are trying to get low on a project, you can also make the call to bring down our cost or margin some. Take care of me when you can, and I will take care of us when we need it."

As it turned out, that is exactly what I did. I became the estimator for Eddie. It was very simple. I did one estimate without any coordination. I was empowered to make the call to close the project. If we had a little extra cushion, then I bumped his estimate proportionately. The speed of business was huge, as was the amount of projects we closed and, eventually, the profit we made. With trust we had expanded profit.

TOOLS

There are two tools I use to give trust and empowerment to others and to turn these qualities into expanded profit. The first is a prescriptive way to delegate that ensures expectations are clear before I empower others. The second tool enables you to enhance and leverage trust through dialogue.

Delegation

Delegation can be one of the most powerful tools on a leader's tool belt. It can be used as a development tool, a recognition tool, and a productivity tool—all at the same time! Most importantly, it can show associates that you trust them.

Why is it that most leaders don't delegate? In my experience, there are three core reasons. Under each of these reasons, I have included a replacement question that can help clarify when you should be delegating and when you shouldn't:

1. **Time:** It is quicker to do it myself.

   Replacement question: Will this task be done multiple times in the future? If so, then I should consider delegation as a timesaving option. It will take more time to delegate the first time, yet a lot of time will be saved if someone else could handle the task in the future.

2. **Quality:** It will not get done to my expectations unless I do it myself.

   Replacement question: Can you ensure the outcome will be great? If so, then document the steps it takes to ensure a quality outcome and go through those steps with the delegate. You need to give trust even when quality is a concern—especially when quality is a concern, because there is more to risk. Giving trust when it is easy has much less of an impact. Giving trust when you have something to lose is huge.

3. **Intent:** It will bother the other person, it is not his or her job, it will send the wrong message, etc.

   Replacement question: Should this task be delegated to others to help them grow, recognize their talent, or even to align tasks that should be their priority rather than yours? If so, then change your mindset. You have the right intent and just need to have the direct-with-respect (DWR) discussion. You need to give trust and most likely your associate will feel good about the delegated task or project if you have the right intent.

An effective delegation of authority hands an able individual work they can effectively execute. The work could be a task or a project. It could be delegated because they currently have all the talent to get it done or because it is a good development of their current skills. Either way, it should follow this process (you will notice that it asks the similar why, what, how questions that we asked in the DWR process):

1. **Why (this is the intent portion of DWR):** Why is this task important? To transfer the commitment you have for the task/project, you need to communicate why it is important. People don't care about the what until they understand the why.

2. **What:** What is it exactly that you need done?

3. **When:** When does it need to be completed? When do you want to hear updates?

4. **How:** How would you like to be updated?

5. **Remind yourself:** The last task is to put a reminder on your calendar or in your tasks. The reminder will ensure that you follow up at the right time to have your expectations met without having to worry about what is going on in the meantime.

Dialogue

Best described in David Bohm's book *On Dialogue*, dialogue is about people engaging in participatory thought. It is a nonjudgmental, nondefensive discussion in which the participants truly listen to each other with the intent of finding the best answers. There are no agendas other than the topic at hand. The participants first seek to understand and then to be understood. Most importantly, the participants feel trusted and have a deeper commitment to what they are doing together. Following are the core attributes of a strong dialogue:

1. **Ideas are not connected to people.** In order to avoid defensiveness or fear, when people state their ideas, keep in mind that their ideas are not connected to them. Ideas immediately become the team's ideas and are open for dialogue. The disconnect between people and ideas allows for openness and freedom of thought.

2. **All seek to understand first.** Without understanding the idea on the table, you cannot add to it effectively.

3. **Move from certainty to curiosity.** When you agree, there is nothing to learn. It is in differences that you can learn something. Others have had different experiences from you and you can learn from their experiences, and they can learn from yours.

4. **Choose a facilitator or leader of the dialogue who is adept at emotional intelligence.** You must be able to recognize when people are becoming connected to the ideas being discussed or when they—either through defensiveness or judgmental statements—are not trying to understand at all.

3

Belief: Associates Own the Culture

HOW MY TEAM PUT ME IN MY PLACE

I thought I was having a nervous breakdown! Two months earlier, I got "the call." Some guy named Tom from corporate called me and said that Jess Newbern, the long-term leader of the Roanoke, Virginia, Trane franchise office, was retiring and that they were looking for someone who could be general manager within three years. I asked, "Why are you calling me?" Tom said, "You are on the list, and we think this is the next best role for you." I told Tom that my family and I were very happy in Huntsville and that we were not moving. If he didn't mind wasting money on a plane ticket for no reason, I would go. He said, "Can you go next week?"

I told Shelby that I was on some list and had to go but that we were not moving. As soon as I walked into the Roanoke office, I felt something different, and it was cool. The people were nice and, oh I don't know, committed? The conversations and interviews were engaging. I was walking back through the airport to my return flight when I called Shelby. "Hey, babe."

"Hey, how did it go?" she asked.

"Well, uh, it was pretty cool," I said.

"Oh, shit! We're moving, aren't we?!"

I decided to take the job because of Jeff Watson, who would be my boss in Roanoke. He and I connected immediately. Our conversations flowed naturally and the topics were things that were important to me. We discussed leadership and people and performance. In fact, although I wrote down a list of pros and cons to help make the decision, this decision seemed to be out of my control. It was almost as if God were moving the chess pieces of my life.

Jeff told me that Jess was selling the Roanoke office and corporate was adding the Richmond office to make Virginia Trane, which he would lead as district manager. He would stay in Roanoke for one year and then move to Richmond, leaving Roanoke in my hands. At the end of the day, I went with my gut and followed Jeff to Roanoke.

In two months, Shelby and I sold our house, purchased a duplex in Roanoke we could live in temporarily, and left our perfect little life in Huntsville, Alabama. At one point, Shelby and I were driving together with the kids in the back of the car when I looked at her and said, "Are we doing the right thing moving to Virginia?" She said, "I think so, yet it would be great if God would give us a sign—and not a small sign." We smiled at each other. Just then a song came on the radio and in unison, we both said, "I really like this song."

"Jinx," I said, and then pushed the button on the receiver to see the title. It was "Meet Virginia" by Train.

Shelby looked at me and said, "That is a pretty big confirmation."

I left on Sunday. I drove dragging a trailer behind me and blew a whole wheel (not just the tire) in the worst part of Chattanooga. Leaving the trailer, which was loaded with my kids' playground equipment (we had added two girls, Sara Catherine and Bailey to our clan) in a deserted gas station, I drove to the closest Lowe's, bought a trailer big enough to carry the other one, and made it back just before the tow truck carried my old trailer away. When I finally arrived at Jeff's house and laid my head on the pillow, it was too much. That was the day I nearly had a nervous breakdown. My heart was beating out of my chest. I was wondering what in the world I had done.

Monday morning was a little better. I was getting excited to start the new adventure. Although I had no idea how to be a general sales manager, I felt that my experience leading the building-automation team in Huntsville had prepared me well. The first day was pretty easy. Saying hi to people as the new boss was pretty cool. I got an office and set up my desk. I also got a new computer.

Tuesday was different. I got to the office early and organized my desk. Then Jeff walked in and said that Jess Newbern had called a meeting of all leaders. Jess had built the strongest culture in the Trane organization bar none. Since the seventies, he had been the franchise holder of Trane's Roanoke office. No one cared much about having the office because Roanoke was such a small town. But over twenty years, Jess built one of the strongest offices in the nation with business performance that rivaled some of the largest cities in North America, including New York, Dallas, and Los Angeles. The business was built on a high-performance culture, which Jess led with passion. He had become legendary within Trane.

I was going to get the opportunity to watch this superhero in action. It was exciting. As soon as I walked into the room, it was clear that it wasn't just managers, all of whom I had met the day before, in the meeting. I later learned that "leaders" in Roanoke included people throughout the organization with high influence and leadership skills.

I still remember sitting on the top-left side of the U-shaped table feeling all alone.

Jess stood and started to speak. "Thanks to all of you for joining the meeting. We are here today to decide if Jeff should move to Richmond next year or next month."

What the hell?! I thought to myself. As my mind was spinning, Jess explained that the culture in Richmond was in desperate need of leadership and that leadership could not be provided remotely. If Jeff stayed in Roanoke another year, it would be a year before the culture work in Richmond started.

Still in a daze, I heard the other leaders start talking. "Jeff should go, we can handle it here," said a woman named Lori.

"It is our job to spread this culture, and we shouldn't wait," said a guy named Dan. There were a few other statements and then the meeting was over. In the blink of an eye, my mentor was leaving in twenty-three days, and I was going to be all alone leading one of the best offices in the nation. Holy shit! How in the world would I do it?!

Fortunately and unfortunately, my youthful confidence took over. Wednesday I met my team and started learning about them and their structure. I also got to meet some customers. On Thursday, my family showed up. On the way to Roanoke, Shelby called and explained it was the worst day of her life because all three kids were in the back of the car screaming in unison, "This is the worst day of our lives!" I held off the nervous breakdown for the second time. The good news was that sixty minutes after they arrived, Shelby was playing bunko with the neighbors (no kidding), and I ended up going to bed alone.

The following Monday, I had my first team meeting. I worked all weekend on a PowerPoint presentation that showed a new direction for our team. It showed that we should organize differently, and after a long weekend of work, I couldn't wait to deliver it to the team. For those of you paying attention, *yes*, I thought it was a good idea to restructure at the beginning of my second week, at the first meeting with my staff.

The presentation landed with a thud. Imagine that! These smart, talented, and experienced people looked at me as if I were speaking a different language. They didn't say anything during the meeting, but afterward they did, and I heard about it. I didn't need 20/20 hindsight to see that I was once again screwing up. Unfortunately, I didn't look back with that hindsight soon enough. Instead, I kept plowing forward. Isn't that what a manager is supposed to do? Managers make decisions and the people must follow. If they don't follow, you're supposed to force them, right? I obviously needed to be a stronger manager to lead the group.

Ever heard the statement, "It's funny to look back on"? Now, this is just what that phase of my life is—funny to look back on. My plowing forward included lots of leadership blunders. I remember team meetings where I did all of the talking—I mean *all* of the talking. My problem-solving technique was to do it all myself. My coaching was short, but not sweet: do it my way. The one thing I had going for me was my intent. I was trying to do the right thing; I just didn't know how to lead yet.

After these mistakes and many more over the next three months, one of the more tenured associates, Gary Seek, came into my office and started explaining that our culture was going the wrong way. He explained that I needed to change if I wanted to save the company. After he left, I slammed the door and called Jeff in a panic. "This place is falling apart. You need to get here immediately." Jeff calmed me down and started to talk me through it.

Just then my cell phone rang. It was Shelby, so I told Jeff I would call him later. She told me that the kids had lice, and I had to get home immediately to check her head.

"I can't, babe, things are crazy here. I can't leave," I told her.

"Get your butt home now. I need you," she said.

"I can't, I am sorry." I hung up. Life was at rock bottom. I was a poor husband, a poor father, a poor boss, and I was obviously no longer in God's chess game. I had to do something different.

The very next day one of the Roanoke leaders, Tammy Swaim, came into my office. She explained that she and a group of others had been discussing their concerns about where the culture was going. They had compiled their thoughts and wanted to run them by me. My paradigms about management were dissipating pretty darn quickly, so I was much more open to listening than I had been in my second week on the job.

Tammy's PowerPoint presentation started with our guiding principles, the behaviors our culture expected of each associate. Then it showed even more specific behaviors that our associates should be displaying if everyone was actually living these guiding principles. Finally, the presentation highlighted where these behaviors were changing, where we were no longer living our guiding principles. I wondered if the changes were recent or if they were long-standing behaviors that needed to be addressed. I was very inquisitive. I wondered what I as a leader could do to influence these behaviors. The dialogue that happened in that moment was powerful. We were leading the company together and holding each other accountable to our responsibility to do so. I was not defensive, and I was working with the team to solve the problem.

After one of the best discussions of my short general-sales-manager career, I went back to my office to think. *What the heck is culture? How do I lead it? How was it built here?* I asked myself. And so on, and so on.

I went to see Lori Wampler, a project manager in our equipment-sales group who had been with the company for a long time. "Hey, what did Jess do when he led this office?" I asked. Lori pulled out a very thick folder with all of Jess's letters. It turns out, he sent a letter to the company an average of five times a year. He also held company meetings at least once a year. Lori had kept all of the letters and agendas. "Read these. They may help you," she said, which is exactly what I did. I also picked up my first leadership book on the way home and started reading it right away.

CULTURE IS OWNED BY THE ASSOCIATES WHO LIVE IN THAT CULTURE

Culture is best defined as "how things get done around here." It is the reason behind the results. It covers how *everything* gets done around a company or a team. For instance, if the leader goes to lunch with the same people every day, then they are his favorites. To get things done under this leader, you must be one of the favorites or you must get one of the favorites to support your idea. If the leader asks for and receives feedback from everyone on staff, then associates in the company will soon claim ownership of the feedback process.

Culture also covers the more important issues such as vision setting, creating strategies, defining annual plans, and executing those plans. Other examples of culture include how your company hires, fires, promotes, recognizes, and rewards people. One final example is teamwork. Whether you think teamwork is important or not, how teams get recognized and rewarded is what truly gets things done. All of these actions and inactions decide how things get done around here, and those getting it done take ownership of it.

How things get done around here can be broken down into the where, what, and how. Since culture is team oriented rather than individual oriented, the culture tells associates where you are going together, what you do together, and how you behave together. This clarity can naturally happen without direction through experience within the culture, or it can be a clearly defined and shared vision (where), mission (what), and guiding principles (how).

The vision explains where the team is going, and the mission explains what they do to get there. The guiding principles connect the company's values to the behaviors we expect of everyone on the team. The guiding principles are the how. Again, these are either defined through natural occurrence (unconscious culture) or they are consciously defined and followed by the team.

From this definition, culture becomes a team's belief system that guides their actions and decisions. (See figure 3.1.)

Culture, by definition, encompasses the beliefs of everyone in that culture—not only the leader's beliefs. Leaders are probably the biggest influencer on culture and can change the culture with enough time. My experience in Roanoke showed that associates—the people who own the culture—are willing to fight for it. And if they are a part of a high-performing culture, they are willing to fight really hard to keep that high level of performance because they feel they have been part of something great and they feel obligated to ensure that it continues.

If a company can build a culture where the associates drive performance and growth from the ground up, a place where candor and feedback is expected and consistent and where passionate customer service is the expectation, then no matter how often leadership changes or associates change roles, the company will sustain a high level of performance.

Figure 3.1: Culture Is a Belief System That Guides Actions

In *Good to Great: Why Some Companies Make the Leap . . . and Others Don't*), author and business icon Jim Collins looked at companies that had achieved great results and sustained them over fifteen years. He then looked at how the companies did this. Three things were consistent across all of the companies: disciplined people, disciplined thought, and disciplined action. In other words, all of the companies had a high-performing culture that did not waver over time. The associates sustained the high-performing cultures because they owned them.

Per our definition, culture is the system of beliefs a group uses to guide their actions and behaviors. Culture is owned and lived by all associates. If a culture is taken to a mature level of candor and commitment, future leaders can actually be grown by the culture. You read that right: great leaders can be raised by a culture rather than the other way around. If leaders have the courage and humility to let high-performing cultures show them how to lead, they can quickly learn how to lead and grow high-performing cultures for other teams. "Level-five leaders," as Collins calls them, have an interesting combination of humility and personal will. They use their humility to listen to the culture while using their will to drive that culture where they want it to go.

My personal experience in Roanoke proves that high-performing cultures can grow a leader. Roanoke held a distribution office for Trane, which was widely considered one of the best in the country, with revenue and profit as large as many much larger cities. In fact, it was often in the top five of operating income against all cities in the country. How was this accomplished? A strong leader named Jess Newbern built a clear definition of the culture he wanted based on a consistent vision, mission, and guiding principles. His leadership changed the culture he stepped into, and once the new culture had been established, the associates claimed ownership of it. When it was time for him to leave, the impact was minimal because Jess didn't own the high-performing culture—the associates did.

After I stepped in, the results continued. In fact, business more than doubled within five years. Obviously, I cannot take credit for the substantial growth. It was the culture. In fact, the culture was now taking my unconscious competency to a conscious level. The culture was teaching me how to lead it. It was by far the best experience of my professional life, and it has allowed me to add value to many other teams and organizations. It is the main reason I wrote this book: to pay forward the blessing of working in a high-performing culture.

THE POLITICS OF BAD CULTURE CAN FIGHT TO WIN

Roanoke Trane is obviously the high-performance side of culture in action. Yet there are negative cultures that are just as passionate about continuing their evil ways. As a member of Roanoke City School Board, I had the fortunate experience of being on a team that completely changed our schools' performance for our kids. Yet, I also had the unfortunate experience of fighting those who only wanted to continue their culture of poor performance. They obviously were not fighting for poorly performing schools; they were fighting to preserve the political system that had created those schools in the first place.

As the school board started to make substantial changes to the system, we had to make some tough decisions. From closing buildings and redistricting to extending school hours and investing in new buildings, the new board and administration were committed to excellence and willing to make the tough decisions necessary to get us there. Yet some city council members fought to keep the previous culture of council-driven change that left the school board without its needed autonomy.

I remember a particular joint meeting between the city council and the Roanoke City School Board during which the tensions between our future state culture and our historic culture hit its peak, and it was all put on display for our community to see. The school board was to report on past decisions, future decisions, and current performance. We were also to discuss the coming budget season.

It took about five minutes for the arrows to start flying. As we were reviewing past decisions, one council member took the floor and said, "I don't trust any of you. You are making horrible decisions for our community and are lying to this council. Your performance is ridiculous, and we need to change out this entire board and administration." My eyes got as big as saucers as I prepared to go to battle. The school board chairman was prepared and immediately stood up, walked to the podium, and began to answer the councilman's "question."

"Mr. Councilman, you have questioned our performance, so I will take the time to answer the question." For the next ten minutes, our chairman reviewed school performance data that existed when this councilman was actually on the school board seven years before and compared it against the current data and trends. About five minutes into the discussion, the councilman interrupted with, "You can throw numbers around, yet we all know—"

Our chairman cut him short: "You asked the question. You will now listen to the answer."

What creates such passionate defense of poor performance? In this case, there was a ton of politics behind the issue, yet at its core there was a commitment to the long-standing culture of the city council controlling the school board. Once the school board decided to step out and achieve excellence, it was counter to that culture, and the councilman was willing to fight for it. Fortunately he was not reelected, and we made some incredible progress together with the more progressive council.

DEFINING YOUR CULTURE IS THE FIRST STEP TO CHANGING IT

Jess and Jeff left me an organization that had a very strong culture. By allowing me to be a part of it, I got to see it and feel it. Eventually, that culture taught me how to lead. The first step to leading the culture was to understand it. As I mentioned, what I learned was that culture was made up of vision (where), mission (what), and guiding principles (how). By defining the where, what, and how, Jess had created culture clarity by defining both current-state and future-state culture. He had defined the culture and set aspirational goals for what the culture could become.

If I were to lead the culture further, I would have to be more aware of how we were living our defined culture and where we were falling short. Once again, it was the associates who taught me this by defining what had changed about our culture since I arrived and what I, as the leader, needed to do about it. They had compared the current state against the definition of the culture and come up with clear shortfalls. They owned the culture by defining where we needed to improve and requiring me to lead the effort with them. All along they used the company's vision, mission, and values as the guideposts.

TOOLS

In a later chapter, we will go into depth about the culture-building process. At this point, I want to provide some awareness of habits that can help you and your associates own a culture of high performance.

Leadership Habits

1. Start all meetings with a culture message.
2. Recognize/reward associates based on culture.
3. Include culture-contribution evaluation in performance reviews.

Leadership Team Habits

1. Include the annual culture review as a part of the planning process.
2. Plan annual culture meetings with all associates.
3. Conduct annual self-evaluation on how the team is leading culture.

Company Systems

1. Use tools and/or surveys to measure the culture annually.

2. Document and automatically facilitate the culture-development process.

3. Ensure that the hiring and onboarding processes are thick with culture.

4

Belief: Leaders Don't Direct, They Lead

HOW THE CULTURE PROCESS SAVED ME, MY TEAM, AND THE COMPANY

That first year after moving from Huntsville as a sales engineer to Roanoke as a general sales manager was the biggest challenge I have faced in my life. As I look back, my biggest struggle was shifting my mindset from an individual contributor to a leader. The experience taught me about culture and challenged every paradigm I had ever had on leadership.

Jess, the longtime franchise leader who built the great culture at Roanoke, first defined culture as "the beliefs of a team that guide their behaviors, actions, and decisions." Jess set clarity around vision, mission, and values, so that there were expectations for those beliefs and resulting behaviors. Jess consistently repeated this theme in almost every letter he wrote and meeting he held.

> Effective communication and commitment to our
> vision and mission encourage active participation and

acceptance of the company philosophy. In effect, success is directly proportional to an organization's efforts to weave their improvement efforts into the basic fabric of the day-to-day business in such a way that those efforts are indistinguishable from "just the way we do business around here." —**Jess Newbern, 1993**

The annual company meetings were almost exclusively about the culture he was trying to create. From reading his letters and some of his personal notes to associates, it was clear that he had strong relationships with his people and very high expectations for these people, for himself, and for the culture.

As soon as I began to understand the importance of culture and high expectations, I started calling Jeff, my current boss who lived in Richmond, almost every morning and talking about culture and how I could lead it. He and I would discuss the books we had recently completed. We would discuss the power of leaders and how they have a huge influence on culture. We would discuss the culture we wanted to have in our teams and how we as leaders could help our associates make it happen. Instead of immediately trying to solve problems in the business, I would think about the impact on culture and the goal of having our associates own that culture. Essentially, I was completely revamping everything I thought about leadership, management, and culture.

It certainly wasn't a sudden change, although over time things started working. The team meetings turned from one-way communication to an open discussion. Even the skeptical people on the team started to reengage. It seemed *we* were making decisions, rather than *me* making decisions. Decision making as a team was much more effective. I was also learning where to be strong—around vision, performance, and culture. Things were starting to flow. I was back in the right game.

One day, about a year after I got to Roanoke, all hell broke loose. In the same day, I received seven phone calls from seven different customers about seven different building-automation projects that were in bad shape. We had problems that ranged from missing deadlines and poor equipment installation to poor communication and programming errors. As soon as I began working on the latest customer complaint, another upset customer would call. The pressure was building, very quickly. Yet something had changed. I was not directing.

I called a team meeting with all leaders involved with these seven projects and ran through the complaints. I then pulled out the culture card that summarized our vision, mission, and values. As we discussed each situation, we realized that we were breaking almost every value and that we were not heading toward our vision. We agreed that this was unacceptable. The team responded immediately by taking responsibility of each project. One owner signed up for each problem with a communication plan. An hour later, the room was empty, and I was ecstatic. For the first time, I was a culture leader. The culture had taught me how to lead it. It wasn't long before the results came as well. We had always been a strong office, with market share as high as 60 percent at times and consistent growth around 10 percent per year. The year after my arrival, we had blown away past results with dramatic revenue growth of 28.9 percent and a market share of 76.9 percent!

LEADERSHIP IS THE LEVERAGE POINT, NOT THE LEVER

The next steps of my career and the beliefs these experiences gave me are proof that it is possible to learn and teach leadership of high-performance cultures. They also reinforced that the leader is the leverage point within the culture. Leaders are responsible for showing a culture where it can go and getting it there. The lever is the culture. The leader supports the culture and takes responsibility to "raise" it. (See figure 4.1.) The leverage point is crucial, yet meaningless without the lever. So it is with leadership. Leadership is crucial to raising culture toward high performance, yet it is only there to serve the culture.

Businesses have many levers to pull to get performance. They can drive revenue through sales or discounts. They can drop costs through layoffs or travel freezes. They can invest in new products or create new features for existing products. They can also decide that local leadership is the key to success and invest in it. So the day-to-day challenges for leaders at any business lie in determining what levers should be pulled to get the best business results.

Businesses use long-range planning and annual operating plans to focus on strategic actions, yet the day-to-day operational pressure is toward the tactical. The pressure to perform today can put the emphasis on levers for short-term-results instead of long-term strategic levers. But the business must make the culture lever its highest priority, and it's up to the leader to maintain that focus.

Businesses are not the only organizations with conflicting pressures between short-term and long-term results. School boards are faced with a very similar situation: how to create the most effective learning environment that gives every child equal opportunity while working with very limited budgets. Similar to business, there is no lack of levers to pull for a school system. Schools can focus on teacher training or better testing or curriculum alignment or attendance rates or graduation rates. In fact, schools may have more options than businesses since they certainly have more opinions coming from the community about what they are doing wrong.

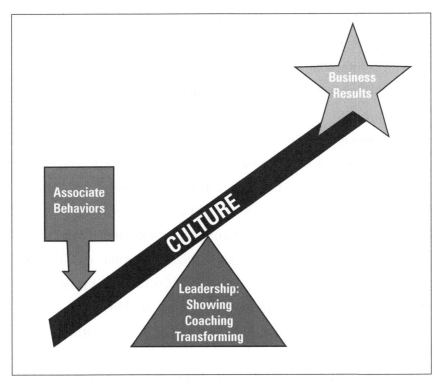

Figure 4.1: Leadership Is the Leverage Point

So, what is a school board to do? For businesses, the leverage point is the leader, and the number-one lever is culture. For school boards, it should be the same. The school leader, the principal, is the leverage point. If school boards and superintendents focus on the principal, they will have the greatest influence on the teachers, parents, and children. In turn, the school boards—via the principals—will have the greatest impact on culture.

If you are a parent, you know exactly what I mean. You can feel the culture of a school as soon as you walk in. A welcoming school secretary, who responds quickly to your request and speaks on the intercom to a teacher, and a teacher who responds in a friendly manner and then sends your child to the front desk so that you can take her to her orthodontist appointment are each proof of a positive culture at work. You feel very comfortable leaving your child in the hands of this school. Or better said, you feel very comfortable leaving your child in the hands of that culture.

The principal is the one person with the most influence to build that perfect school environment. The principal is the leverage point for school districts. The principal can set clear expectations, hire the right teachers and provide them the right coaching, recognize poor performers, ensure the execution of core curriculum, and define proper processes. A great principal will show what is possible, coach toward that goal, and lead the transformation. This is just like a general sales manager deciding which salespeople to hire, coaching them on joint sales calls, holding them accountable for poor sales performance, and defining the proper sales process.

Roanoke City Schools in Roanoke, Virginia, is just such a case. They have focused on getting the right people as principals, giving them the training they need to be strong leaders, and providing the tools required for creating high-performance cultures. Their success is proof that leadership is the leverage point. A deeply urban school district with poverty rates above 67 percent as measured by free and reduced-cost lunch recipients, the district had a dismal graduation rate of around 50 percent, and more than 40 percent of the district's schools were unaccredited. Within a three-year period of finding the right principals and training them, the graduation rate rose, astonishingly, to above 80 percent, with 100 percent of schools accredited! This would be like a business in a depressed market growing its overall profit by 65 percent with all of its employees being in the top 25 percent of performance.

These results are almost unheard of for public schools. How in the world could a public education system that has been in place for decades achieve such an unparalleled improvement in results in such a short timeframe? There are many, many other things the school district did to achieve these amazing results, yet at the core of many of their discussions and actions was the leadership leverage point. For our work, it is the leverage point of leaders who moved the lever of a high-performing culture. It is about culture and leadership.

Roanoke City Schools is not the only data point to demonstrate this belief. In their book, *Influencer: The Power to Change Anything*, Kerry Patterson, Joseph Grenny, David Maxfield, Ron McMillan, and Al Switzler tell the story of a company that sent hundreds of its employees through training to help them increase productivity. The process was a major financial investment, and the company expected a return. Yet, after the training, there was very little change in productivity.

They searched for what failed by interviewing the associates who went through the training. They found that although the training was well done, the actual productivity results depended on the leader. Consistently, the associates had three issues: (1) leaders shot down their productivity-improvement ideas, so they stopped sharing these ideas; (2) leaders did not hold associates' peers accountable in getting the productivity ideas done, which sent the message that productivity was not really important; and (3) leaders did not take feedback well. The leaders were not leveraging the training to achieve higher productivity. Actually, it was exactly the opposite. Although the company had invested in the lever of training, they did not have the leverage point of a leader to drive performance higher in the day-to-day business environment. The lever was on flat ground.

Interestingly enough, while they were trying to find out why the training wasn't working, they also found places where it was working.

In these places, they found different leaders. And guess what? People felt like their ideas were heard, their peers were held accountable, and the leaders took feedback well. These places are examples of how leadership was leading rather than directing. Leaders were the leverage point for the lever of training, and the business results followed.

PEOPLE LEAVE THEIR LEADERS, NOT THEIR COMPANIES

If someone leaves a company, there is a good chance that they don't like their leader and are not in a great culture. Maybe the best way to see how your organization achieves leadership as a leverage point is to look at leadership failure and why people leave companies. In his blog, www.johndehartblog.com, John DeHart reported on a *New York Times* article about how Google went about discovering why its employees left.[1] Google's found, in effect, three primary reasons:

1. They are not connected to the mission or purpose of the organization. (This is the why behind the what.)

2. They don't like their coworkers.

3. They don't like their bosses.

So, the first reason is connection to mission, and the second reason is peers. Ask yourself, who is most influential in translating the mission into an employee's role? And who is most influential in hiring, training, holding accountability, and replacing employees in a company? That's

---

1. Adam Bryant, "Google's Quest to Build a Better Boss," *New York Times*, March 12, 2011, accessed September 20, 2012, http://www.nytimes.com/2011/03/13/business/13hire.html.

right: the leader. So, Google's study essentially says that the top three reasons are about a leader being the leverage point.

Since poor leadership is the big reason for departures, it stands to reason that the opposite is true as well. Good leaders are the leverage point of a great culture. Said another way, if you don't get leadership right, it will be tough to get the culture-development process right. Google's study confirms this as well. Google also studied its high-performing associates and have found one thing in common with all of them. They were led by a great leader. Great leaders have teams with more high performers and better performance overall. What a surprise!

Effective leaders connect their people to the vision and mission of the company and place a high standard on performance. They discuss the why before the what. They *show* why being at the company is important and they provide a mission for what they and the organization's employees could do together. Then, effective leaders *coach* many associates to high performance, and help the rest to achieve their best. In the end, people will like their peers because their peers are best at what they do. Through these efforts, effective leaders *transform* the organization to a high-performance culture.

EXCELLENCE IS POSSIBLE EVEN UNDER PRESSURE

Leaders lead. They show people what is possible. They coach on how to achieve the goals they set. They transform the culture, knowing all the while that the associates own the culture. Said another way, effective leaders place a high standard on culture, and they lead people to it. They make excellence cultural so that the associates can then lead it.

This reminds me of a discussion I had with my eight-year-old daughter on the way to ballet class. The class was across town, and we always seemed to be cutting it close to getting her there on time. One day, we were running late, and I said, "Sara, we are going to make it right on time." She looked at me and said, "Daddy, early is on time, on time is late, and late is unacceptable." A huge, prideful smile crossed my face. Sara conveyed that she understood the definition of excellence and could provide a clear vision of what it looked like.

In this context, excellence is defined as the pursuit of the highest standard. Yet excellence is not perfection, and there is a *big* difference between the two. Using Sara's definition, excellence would be getting to ballet five minutes early almost every time. Perfection would be getting there exactly five minutes early, five days a week, fifty-two weeks a year for twenty years.

Since perfection is nearly impossible, it is deflating in nature. You or someone you know has probably experienced a boss who had expectations that were unachievable. The boss was never happy because she always expected an unreachable standard to be met. Of course, it was frustrating and demoralizing. Yet, it is just as frustrating to be led by a pushover. The team of a pushover boss becomes lackadaisical.

Great leaders aim for excellence, which is the middle ground between perfection and pushover. Great leaders are excited about improvement and desire to become better. They celebrate success, yet they are never really satisfied with the current state.

To lead a culture to excellence, great leaders must break the culture down into two segments: (1) setting the right goals (show), and (2) leading those goals (coach). Great leaders care enough to set goals with thought and reason. They set goals that are best in class, yet clearly achievable. They know that they are setting the right target for the culture and the associates within that culture.

Once great leaders set the goals, they spend all of their energy leading those goals. Once they know where the culture lever can go, they spend all of their energy becoming the leverage point. They recognize that there will be a lot of tension between where the culture is versus where the goals suggest it can be. Our leadership leverage point realizes that it is just that tension that will raise the culture lever higher.

In his book, *The Fifth Discipline: The Art & Practice of the Learning Organization*, Peter Senge describes the gap between current reality and the vision we hold for ourselves as a "creative tension." He describes this tension as a rubber band stretched between two hands. One hand represents the vision and the other the current state. The rubber band is the tension that tries to pull the two together. For a culture leader, that tension is between the current state and the goal of excellence.

Leadership as a leverage point is the process for ensuring that the creative tension pulls toward excellence. Great leaders set excellence as the standard and focus almost all of the creative tension on moving the culture toward that goal. When pressured, associates will use their creativity to get out of the tension. Great leaders make sure that every associate's creativity is focused solely on achieving excellence, versus protecting the current state.

One of my favorite examples of leadership using the tension to drive excellence was the Roanoke MS Dinner of Champions, which is an event held every year across the nation to raise donations for multiple sclerosis by honoring individual leaders in communities across the county. Since its inception in 1972, the dinner has become one of the country's most popular recognition events, successfully increasing donations every year. But this year the outlook was grim. The economy had taken a dramatic downturn, and the traditional contributors were strapped for cash. Across the country, the goal was to avoid dropping below the previous year's level. Most organizations came in under the previous year's results.

Whereas many committees used their creative tension to pull toward the current state by giving all the reasons why the goal should be lower, the Roanoke MS Dinner of Champions committee used their creative tension to pull toward a stronger vision. Their vision was different because they decided that there was no better time for people to get involved, for contributions to increase for the needy, and for communities to work together for a greater purpose.

They then went to work to achieve their goal. They used weekly meetings, new marketing pieces, common elevator speeches, monthly adjustments to plan based on weekly feedback, and mid-event brainstorming sessions to keep the tension toward the vision. Long story short, in one of the toughest environments, they blew away the previous year's total contribution.

To achieve excellent results like this requires showing, coaching, and transforming. A leader shows what is possible through a clear vision of excellence. The leader is resolute that the vision of excellence can be achieved and that the team can do it. The leader certainly must listen to the issues and gather additional input, but he must continue to keep the "vision hand" in place, so that the creative tension pulls up.

With the vision of excellence in place, the leader must do lots of coaching. Pessimism and skepticism exist in every team. The leader uses these voices as input and coaches these individuals on where their energy is better placed. The coach explains that individual and team growth is what really matters. The coach asks all team members to minimize their blame and justification while spending the majority of their energy on how they can achieve together. The coach also asks for those on board to help those who are still on the fence to gain complete team commitment.

The team watches the leader's every step, every day. The leader needs to continually and enthusiastically recommunicate why the vision is so important and how he believes the team can achieve its desired goals. The leader must celebrate small wins that show progress. The leader must see disappointments as yet another learning opportunity that will eventually take the team to its goal. It is this positive spirit that solidifies the team's commitment.

Through clear vision setting and consistent coaching toward goals, a leader can transform a culture. And leaders who transform a culture are themselves transformed. They are part of the process, and they are influenced by it. Those leaders have learned how to function as even better leverage points next time.

TOOLS

Great leaders lead rather than direct. They show their team what is possible through a clear vision and through their actions and decisions. They lead with their feet. Then, they focus their energy on coaching the team toward what is possible, keeping a high standard for results and using the creative tension to achieve that bar. Finally, their vision and coaching transform the culture as they themselves transform. At the end of the day, leaders are a part of the team and are thus leading themselves as they are leading others.

Next are three tools to help leaders lead. The first, the three questions, is focused on the combination of associates owning culture and leaders leading rather than directing. This tool can help leaders facilitate organizational learning (showing them what to do and coaching them on how to do it). The second tool, 360 feedback, is focused squarely on leaders leading by example. It is a common tool in business today, yet here we are using it from a leadership perspective. The final tool, personal-development plans (PDPs), is about helping leaders become better coaches. It is a form that facilitates stronger dialogues about personal-development planning.

Three Questions

To build a strong culture, there must be trust between associates and leaders. There must also be trust between each associate on the team. Unfortunately, managers often get in the way of trust by using their natural problem-solving skills. They tend to get in the middle of conflict and problems to solve them, rather than ensuring that the associates solve them directly with each other. This is a prime example of leaders directing rather than leading.

Instead of getting in the middle of associate conflict, managers should use the three questions tool to make sure trust is actually enhanced and associates are involved in the conflict-and problem-solving process. Ask associates these three questions:

1. **Have you spoken with the other associate(s) directly?**

    a. If the answer is no, say, "Please leave my office and speak with them directly about your concerns. If I get in the middle right now, I will only harm trust and teamwork. Before you leave, I have two more questions."

    b. If the answer is yes, say, "Great. Thanks for taking that step. I am happy to be a sounding board at this point. How did it go?"

2. **Have you considered what you did to contribute to this conflict?** Explain that until we are honest with ourselves and

approach problems with a 100%–0% attitude, we cannot ask others to do the same. Therefore, start with yourself. This also helps you walk into the discussion open and listening.

3. **Have you thought about potential solutions to this conflict?** Explain that the only intent of your conversation should be to find the best solution. To make sure you are walking in with the right intent, start by asking what possible solutions to the problem exist.

By using these three questions, leaders help associates deal with conflict directly, solve problems, and build trust and teamwork in the process.

360 Feedback

The 360-feedback tool gathers feedback from direct reports, peers, and superiors for every leader in the organization. The tool allows for confidentiality (the person giving feedback remains anonymous if they wish).

The opinions of our associates and customers about our leadership and company performance must be constantly requested, heard, and acted upon. Associates are the ones who have the best advice on what is right and wrong with a company because they are the ones who live within the processes and deal with the customers daily. Associates own the culture and should be included in providing feedback on how it is working. As soon as the leader thinks she doesn't need feedback, it is a sure sign that her team or company is on a downward slide.

Therefore, you should set processes in place to ensure feedback is received and acted upon. That feedback should be for individual leaders and the company at large. It should happen at least once annually. The good news is that these processes do not have to be extravagant. It can be as easy as six questions in a Word document that you email to your team. The team could offer feedback in a reply email or write it up, print it out, and put it in your mailbox if they want to remain anonymous.

Here are six example questions:

1. What should I/we continue doing?

2. What should I/we start doing?

3. What should I/we stop doing?

4. What is my/our greatest strength?

5. What is my/our greatest development area?

6. What other comments would you like to make about me/our company?

Closing the loop is a crucial step if you want to be successful with the feedback process. The person or company receiving feedback must reply to those who gave the feedback with a summary of what they heard and the actions they are going to take as a result of the feedback. Without this step, the associates or customers will not feel like they were heard or that their feedback added any value. The next time they are asked, they will be less likely to get involved.

Although 360-feedback tools are quite common, it is less common for leaders to use the tool to gather feedback from their direct reports. But this is a crucial process for leaders to lead effectively. If a leader is constantly looking for feedback and holding himself accountable to acting on that feedback, he is leading the rest of the team to do the same. He is leading with his actions by saying, "I am not perfect. I need your feedback to grow. I want to improve my service to you."

When a leader leads with the 360-feedback process, it is very easy to ask associates to do the same. It's an example of the leader leading rather than directing.

Personal-Development Plans (PDPs)

Personal-development plans allow leaders to create their individual development plans based on the feedback they have received. Each plan should include the development plan for one strength and one weakness. This is a crucial point. Everyone—leaders and the people they lead—should be expected to develop their strengths as well as their weaknesses. There are generally three categories of development: "on the job," "coach," and "outside training." On the job should account for 70 percent of the development, 20 percent should include a coach, and 10 percent should be in the form of outside training.

The Leadership Competencies form is used to ensure that there is a strong dialogue between a leader and her manager. (See figure 4.2.) Both the leader and manager should fill out the form on their own and then get together to discuss their ratings and thoughts. The form makes it easy to hold a valuable discussion through a three-part process. Before we go through the process though, let's understand the form a little better.

First, take a look at the competencies. They are divided into two sections: S and T, for skills and talents. There is no solid black line between these; the intention is to separate those things you are born with (talents) versus those you have developed over time (skills). The main reason for the separation is that if someone rates poorly on a bunch of talents, he may be in the wrong role.

Second, look at the proficiency scale (figure 4.3), which allows for a rating between 0 and 8. Notice that there is a title and description for each rating. It is important to realize that a "4" is not a bad score as it

Competency	Include Y/N	Importance Rating (1–8)	Rating (1–8)
S – Business Knowledge			
S – Composure			
S – Decision Quality			
S – Direct with Respect (assertive)			
S – Listening			
S – Influence Skills			
S – Organizing and Prioritizing			
S – Planning			
S – Problem Solving			
S – Self-awareness			
T – Action Oriented/Energy			
T – Building High-performance Teams			
T – Creativity (Innovative)			
T – Developing Others			
T – Ethics and Values			
T – Interpersonal Skills			
T – Managing Vision/Purpose			
T – Perseverance			
T – Results based/Commit to Excel (High Standards)			
T – Strategic			

Figure 4.2: Leadership Competencies

Scale Level Value	Scale Level Label	Description
0	Cannot Evaluate	Not Required/Unknown
1	Some Familiarity, No Proficiency	Heard of it, know the function/behavior
2	Some Familiarity, Minimal Proficiency	Have used the function/behavior once. Need training to gain proficiency. Cannot perform without assistance.
3	Familiar, Need Assistance Often	Have used the function/behavior in the past—need training and often need assistance to perform.
4	Familiar, Sometimes Need Assistance	Have used the function/behavior in the past and sometimes need assistance to perform.
5	Familiar, Do Not Need Assistance	Use the function/behavior and do not need assistance to perform most of the time.
6	Proficient	Proficient in the function/behavior—can perform.
7	Proficient and Can Assist Others	Proficient in the function/behavior—others ask me for assistance.
8	Proficient and Can Teach	Proficient in the function/behavior—can teach others and serve as a role model.

Figure 4.3: Proficiency Scale

indicates someone who is familiar with the skill/talent, yet sometimes needs some help. (Don't we all need help sometimes?)

Now, let's go through the three-step process. First, decide if the skill or talent should be included with this evaluation. Decide yes or no based on the importance of the skill or talent for the role you are evaluating. Next, rate the importance for each skill and talent that you included in the ratings under the "Importance" column. Finally, evaluate the individual ratings for each of the skills or talents that you rated greater than 5.

Use this tool to create strong dialogues with your boss about your personal strengths and development areas. Also use this tool with your direct reports to help them identify their strengths and development areas. Again, once you are done with the competency dialogue, you should choose the number-one strength and number-one development area for personal development in the coming year. Important: make sure to include strengths—not just weaknesses—in the development plan.

You should then rate the competency of leading your guiding principles. I've used the Trane guiding principles as an example. (See figure 4.4.) The point of rating is to remind you and the leaders you work with of the importance of you leading the guiding principles. Leaders should lead!

GP	Description	Rating
1	Respect – Safety, trust, urgency, diversity.	
2	Integrity – Do the right thing, quality, accountability.	
3	Teamwork – Total team, recognize, have fun, earn empowerment.	
4	Innovation – Positive mental attitude, openness, culture of continuous improvement.	
5	Courage – Direct with respect, embrace change, calculated risks.	

Figure 4.4: Guiding Principles

5

Belief: Everyone Wants to Grow, Serve, and Perform

PEOPLE AREN'T NAILS, SO LEADERS SHOULDN'T BE HAMMERS

I changed my role as a sales engineer in Huntsville, Alabama, to a general sales manager in Roanoke, Virginia. As a general sales manager in Roanoke, I had learned the importance of culture and leadership. I had also changed my whole mindset on what it took to be a great leader. After I learned that culture was the lever to excellence and leadership was the leverage point, it was time to practice being the leverage point. Being promoted to general manager was the perfect opportunity to give it a shot. I was responsible for three locations and 150 associates. The general manager role was much more than selling HVAC equipment. We led building automation, service, parts, and contracting as well. The role also meant leading all of the functional roles, including HR, finance, and IT.

Since my background was mainly sales with a bit of building automation, I had a lot to learn. Running a service department was foreign to me, as was managing service technicians. The technicians were talented people who serviced and fixed all of the Trane equipment throughout our territory, so they were away from the office most of the time. I also was expected to lead two parts stores, which were more like retail businesses and even more foreign to me.

Though I didn't really know much about the company that I was supposed to manage, I was calm and ready to handle challenges. I wasn't really sure why, yet I knew it had to do with culture and leadership. The stressful part was the challenge of leading a great team. Starting this new concept of leadership as the leverage point with a high-performing culture was a big deal. I could figure out the business specifics, but could I lead the high-performance culture to a new level of excellence? There was no time like the present to figure it out. *Let's get the team together*, I thought.

The leaders were from very diverse areas of the company and included engineers, technicians, salespeople, and retail managers. I liked every one of them. They worked well together, knew about culture, and were good leaders. Yet, the culture hadn't reached a magical pinnacle. There was just something in my gut that said we could be more.

For instance, the largest customer of our parts business was our service department. It makes sense if you think about it. Our service business probably fixed more Trane equipment than any other service company in the area and, therefore, bought more Trane parts than any other service company. Yet, the parts leader and service leader did not act like partners. They were more like individual business leaders who were nice to each other.

It also bothered me that our discussions around people were mainly about discipline and hard work. These are critical characteristics of any successful person, but they form only one small piece of the pie. It seemed our people leadership was one- or two-dimensional.

At this point, I was unconsciously competent about this culture thing, which is to say that I had some natural talent to lead culture, but it wasn't a honed skill. Inside me I had a tension between what we were and what we could be. Our culture was grand, but it could be so much more. We talked about getting better every day while also guarding the culture we had. The lessons I had recently learned were driving me to find the next phase, though I didn't yet know what that next phase was.

At this point, I was getting better at leading meetings rather than directing meetings, but I still fell back on my bad behaviors (and I still do to this day). One of our sales engineers, Jeff Wolfe, was not meeting my expectations, and I decided to talk to him about it in front of his peers during our monthly sales meeting. When he challenged me, I challenged him right back and "won" the argument. It wasn't pretty.

When the meeting was over, I could see that Jeff was upset. I walked (or should I say "strutted") over to check in on him. He looked at me and said, "To a hammer, everything is a nail. The problem is there are no nails in this room." The awkward silence seemed to last forever. Then he walked out the door.

Normally, I would take someone to lunch after our monthly sales meeting. This time I walked out the front door and headed to a restaurant by myself. Jeff's comment stung, and I needed to think through what he said. The defensive part of me thought that Jeff was oversensitive, that he had trouble with candid discussions. But I had a stronger feeling that he was right. I did not respect people at times. I also tended to be more focused on what I was trying to achieve rather than what they really needed. When Jeff said, "There are no nails in this room," he was sending me the message that everyone in that room wanted to be successful. They didn't need a hammer because they already had the desire to be great.

The "aha!" happened as I was paying my check at lunch. In two sentences, Jeff challenged my assumptions about people by saying that everyone wants to be great and they desire the help to get there. The problem was that I knew how to be a hammer, but I didn't know how to help people be great. This thought stayed in the front of mind as I was promoted to general manager.

I did not know how to help people be great. When I looked back on my success and failures in leadership so far, it was my desire for feedback and willingness to grow from that feedback that drove my growth. For instance, when I first arrived in Roanoke and our project administrator Tammy came to me with her team's concerns, it was my listening that developed a new awareness. It was my willingness to change that allowed for something different. That is when I transformed from director to leader. I needed to help all leaders learn what I had learned about feedback and personal change.

When I first read about emotional intelligence—in Daniel Goleman's *Emotional Intelligence: Why It Can Matter More Than IQ*—I realized that it was the key to getting our leaders, team, and culture to the next level. Emotional intelligence focuses on self-awareness, self-control, relationship awareness, and relationship management. The book explores in depth the importance of self-awareness in becoming a great leader. I thought back to the great mentors of my past, people like my favorite professor in college, Dr. Simon, who always challenged me. When I challenged him back, he would listen and sometimes even change his opinion. Another great leader was my manager, Jeff Watson, in Roanoke. Both of these leaders had an amazing combination of humility and confidence. They had great self-awareness.

The vivid images of those two hit home with me. I decided that self-awareness was a critical component to personal development and that personal development had something to do with helping people be great in the next phase of our culture. In my action-oriented style, I decided to start my own leadership/personal-development class. After working on the format and agenda for a couple of months, I was ready to give it a try. I gathered some managers on my team, as well as a few other "leaders," and pulled them together for our first meeting.

The concept was to triangulate three "lenses" of feedback so that all participants could get a clear image of their strengths and weakness. The first lens was feedback from their classmates, the second lens was feedback from their peers, and the third lens was learning about their natural social style. The class started with an open dialogue on leadership, which eventually led to the team choosing their top ten characteristics of a leader.

As homework, every participant rated themselves and each of the other participants from 1 to 10 on each of the ten characteristics. They also listed the top and bottom characteristic for each person. In the next class, every participant stood up and went through their self-ratings. Then we went around the table with all participants telling how they rated that person, including the top and bottom characteristics. It was intense.

In true Roanoke style, these leaders drank every sip of the development process. In fact, they constantly made it better by providing suggestions for improvement after every class. Because it was a pilot program, they felt obligated to make it better for the next group. At the end of the six-month program, we had really created something cool. It was time for the graduation, during which every leader would display their personal lessons and plans for ongoing personal development.

There have been multiple times where something life changing has happened to me. Shelby saying yes when I asked her to marry me was one of those times. The births of Alex, Sara, and Bailey were three other fabulous moments. The graduation of the inaugural personal-development class was another one of those moments. I was almost in tears multiple times as every leader talked emotionally about what the class had meant to them. Their personal growth was real and powerful. They had more self-awareness than ever before, and it was because their teammates had the courage to speak up. They seemed ready to make substantial changes in their lives. They were focused on being great and learning how to get there.

That's when it hit me. This was the answer to the hammer question. I could see how I could help people be great. Every person in that development class found the class powerful because they all found clarity on what was special about them and what they needed to do to grow. Once they saw their uniqueness, they were clearer about how it could be used to make a difference for others. And clearer still about how they could be the best at something. By finding and articulating an individual's strengths and development areas, we had identified what made them special. By talking about tangible ways they could grow these talents, the participants became excited about the future. And, by connecting those unique qualities to how they could serve others, the participants felt a real purpose. We had identified how what made them special could do great things for others.

For example, Tom, one of the participants, was an analytical person by nature and saw himself as a leader. The class taught him that his technical competence and analytical style were extremely valuable to the company. It allowed him to make great decisions for our customers. At the same time, he had a weak connection to people. People thought he was so analytical that he didn't care about the people side of the business. They felt Tom was treating them like a task rather than as a human when they were with him. From this awareness, Tom went to work becoming the leader he could be by taking Dale Carnegie training classes and reading books on emotional intelligence. A survey six months later showed he had dramatically improved his people skills and was ready to lead. Tom's ability to combine a natural analytical style with a connection to people made him great at what he did as a leader of technical people. In fact, he was confident that he could be one of the best at what he did.

Scott, on the other hand, took a different route. He was our controller at the time and was proud of his ability to find business answers in the numbers. He tended to stay in the office and number crunch, because he was good at it. But the feedback told him that he had strong people skills, values, and a positive attitude. His uniqueness was the combination of business answers and people skills. If he could improve his focus on action, he could be a great leader of people. This was an awakening for Scott because he had never seen himself in that light. He worked on his action orientation and then asked his boss to add people management to his responsibilities. He blossomed as a leader and soon found that he could be one of the best leaders in our company. Eventually, Scott switched roles altogether and ended up leading a team of people for an entirely different business.

My understanding of the philosophical shift that Tom, Scott, and the other leaders in the class represented developed over time. Once I had thought my job as a manager was to continually increase the performance of all the people on our team or get rid of them if they were not making the cut. My approach was to get work done through people. After the personal-development class, I realized that I had it all wrong, and I shifted my definition of leadership to "getting people done through work." Although I certainly wanted every person to be at his or her best, I had it all wrong. It is a slight shift in words, yet a huge shift in mentality when we change the definition of leadership to *getting people done through work*. When you focus on the people getting the work done and ask yourself as a leader how you can help them be great through their work—rather than focusing on the work and asking how the people can make the work great—you find true leadership.

What does it take to get people done through work? As I learned in the class, you first have to know the person. You need to know what their natural strengths are and how you can grow those strengths to make them even stronger. The goal is to instill in them a strong feeling of importance and power about what they already have. With the clarity of their newfound power, the graduates immediately began to use their strengths in new ways, where that power could make a difference for others. Finally, as they connected the dots from strength to service, they looked for greatness. They measured the results and through those results found new ways to grow.

My job as a leader had completely changed. Instead of driving performance, my job was to help my associates identify their strengths and then support their growth of those strengths. Then, as their leader, I had an obligation to make sure those strengths were in a place to be maximized. Finally, I needed to be candid about the results (performance). If people were failing, it was most likely one of two reasons. Either we had not clearly defined their strengths, or they were in a professional role where they could not use their strengths, where they could not be successful. My job as a leader was to help people find their individual purpose and align that with the purpose they served in our company. Yes, it ended in performance, and that is a complete mind shift from where I was before this revelation.

In my early years in Roanoke, leadership was about directing. Through bumps and bruises, I learned that leadership was about leading. As I crossed a major chasm, moving from "me" to "we," I learned that leadership was also about helping talented people find their purpose. I learned that great leaders are great facilitators of talent, and the goal is to place that greatness where it serves best.

PURPOSE IS THE GREATEST OF THE THREE MOTIVATORS

People often talk about motivating employees as being one of a leader's key responsibilities. A leader can play a large role in helping people increase their motivation by helping them align their talents with their role in the business.

The three great motivators of people are fear, incentive, and purpose. It's obvious why the first two are motivators. Fear means "I will fire you if you do not get this done." Incentive means "I will pay you if you get this done." Daniel Pink, in his book *Drive: The Surprising Truth about What Motivates Us*, calls these extrinsic motivators. The vast majority of managers in business today use these two motivators. However, the most powerful and only sustainable motivator is *purpose*.

Purpose is an internal motivator. Being driven by a purpose that seems like destiny creates personal motivation that thrives and survives much greater and longer than the motivation created by fear or incentive. If you feel that you have a special quality and that this quality is serving a greater good, then you will constantly think and work on what you are trying to accomplish. If you believe what you do makes a real difference and that you are one of the best at doing it, the external motivators are really only bonuses.

Believing that people want to grow, serve, and perform is the same as believing that the greatest motivator of people is purpose. Personally, I believe that we are all here for a reason and that we have been given gifts to fulfill that purpose. Leaders have the opportunity to help each associate achieve their purpose while not knowing exactly what that purpose might be. This paradoxical yet noble goal was stated perfectly by the Hebrew existentialist philosopher Martin Buber and quoted in Peter Senge's book, *The Fifth Discipline*:

> The only thing that can become fate for man is belief in fate. The free man is he who wills without arbitrary self-will. He believes in destiny, and believes that it stands in need of him. It does not keep him in leading strings, it awaits him, he must go to it, yet does not know where it is to be found. But he knows that he must go out with his whole being. The matter will not turn out according to his decision; but what is to come will come only when he decides on what he is able to will. He must sacrifice his puny, unfree will, that is controlled by things and instincts, to his grand will, which quits defined for destined being.
>
> Then, he intervenes no more, but at the same time he does not let things merely happen. He listens to what is emerging from himself, to the course of being in the world; not in order to be supported by it but to bring it to reality as it desires.

A LEADER HELPS PEOPLE GROW, SERVE, AND PERFORM

Leaders must first believe that each individual has a unique combination of skills and talents and that it is his job to make sure individuals *grow* those skills and talents. Leaders must also believe that these talents, if put in the right situation or role, have the opportunity to *serve* others in a great way, thus helping people be great through service to customers and the company. Finally, leaders must believe that the only way to be fair to people is to hold them accountable to the *performance* or results they are achieving. With a grow, serve, perform (GSP) mentality, leaders are getting people done through work. (See figure 5.1.)

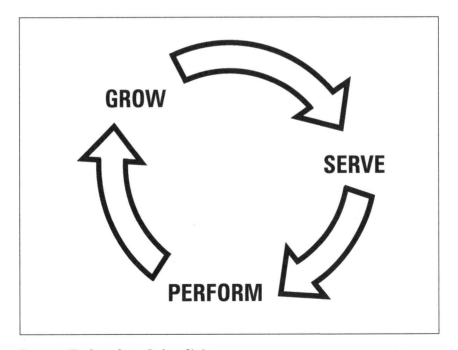

Figure 5.1: The Grow, Serve, Perform Circle

Grow

First things first: each associate in the company has a unique set of skills or talents. Do you believe this as a leader? Do you go into your performance reviews with a search for strengths? Or do you tend to look for weaknesses? By recognizing natural talents and abilities, you send the message that associates are important and vital. You send the message that you want them in the company because of what is great about them and that you want to help them develop their strengths.

Serve

Once the strengths are identified, the leader's job is to help the associate serve a role for the company with those strengths. They could be serving customers, other associates, or even the manager. The point is that they are making a difference with their unique strengths.

People are more likely to take even a mundane job if they are also given the opportunity to do what they love. The leader should work hard to provide options, like task forces, additional projects, and special assignments that allow the individual to use his or her unique set of talents and skills.

Perform

Your business must have results. They define the greatness of people and the business. Results are also the indicators for further growth. They complete the circle. Strong leaders talk candidly about individual results because they know it is the right thing to do for the company and the individual.

LEADERS LEAD WITH INTENT

As leaders prepare for a direct-with-respect discussion, the number-one question they should ask themselves is, "What is my intent?" If their intent is to have an open discussion with the associate to find the right answer, they are spot on. If, on the other hand, their goal is to find fault or prove themselves right or to force action, then the discussion will be direct, yet it will most likely not be with respect. Leaders cannot show respect for their associates' thoughts and opinions if they come in with preconceived notions about how the discussion should turn out. Said another way, if leaders are open to all possible answers, then they should feel very comfortable asking even the toughest of questions.

GSP is circular. Once you look at the performance for what it is— alignment of skills and behaviors—you create plans for changing or adding new skills and behaviors for better performance next time. By being candid about results and discussing those results openly, you learn something that allows you to grow once again. And that growth will enable you to serve even better the next time, therefore leading to better results.

In *First, Break All the Rules: What the World's Greatest Managers Do Differently*, authors Marcus Buckingham and Curt Coffman list twelve questions that identify the level of a company based on what the associates see as important. Similar to Maslow's hierarchy of needs, Buckingham and Coffman's work identifies four levels:

1. **Base camp:** What do I get?
2. **Camp 1:** What do I give?
3. **Camp 2:** Do I belong here?
4. **Camp 3:** How can we all grow?

These camps follow the concept of GSP perfectly. If a company has no concept of GSP and puts very little effort into identifying strengths, the people are probably mired in the "What do I get?" stage. Once a company starts to discuss strengths and roles, the associate moves to the "What do I give?" stage. As the GSP application matures, the associate moves to the "Do I belong here?" stage, which is similar to self-actualization for Maslow's hierarchy. Finally, at full maturity, the entire team takes on the GSP approach and starts to ask the grander question, "How can we all grow?"

As described in *First, Break All the Rules*, Gallup interviewed the associates in over 2,500 business units, representing twelve different industries, using the twelve questions that identify the four levels. When they combined the results of the survey with business results of each business unit, they found some compelling evidence. The employees who responded positively to the twelve questions were part of organizations that had much higher business results.

And there was another finding in their analysis. The business units within a company had different scores as well. The different scores correlated to the individual business unit's business performance. In other words, Belief #4, "Leaders Don't Direct, They Lead," combined with Belief #5, "Everyone Wants to Grow, Serve, and Perform" directly correlates with much better business results.

STRONG ENGAGEMENT ACHIEVES EXCELLENT RESULTS

It is worth going deeper into why the connection between business results and the GSP approach is so strong. To do that, let's play pretend for a minute. Pretend that you are an associate in a company that cares about you. They help you identify your talents and they invest in your growth. Your boss was one of the people who helped you identify those talents and is also one of your trusted advisors in growing those talents. He and your peers constantly put you in roles and responsibilities that use those talents. You are very clear on the results you are achieving because you get constant feedback, both positive and negative. One thing is very consistent: the feedback is always used as a growth mechanism.

Are you engaged in your work in this pretend world? Of course you are! Engagement means that you feel passionate about what you are doing and why you are doing it. Because it is important to you, you are fully vested. It feels like your purpose.

For those new to the subject, associate engagement is defined as the extent to which an employee is committed, rationally and emotionally, to the objectives of the organization. From this definition, it is clear that the purpose created from a grow/serve/perform culture will certainly drive high associate engagement. Studies have shown the following to be true for associate engagement:

1. Companies with strong versus weak engagement have a growth over five years of 62 percent versus 21 percent.

2. Companies with strong versus weak engagement are more likely to keep their employees for at least two years (95 percent versus 34 percent) even for less pay (93 percent versus 10 percent).

3. Engaged employees are 45 percent more likely to stay.

GREG LEAVES THE COMPANY TO SERVE HIS PURPOSE

Sometimes when I talk to people about GSP, they ask what should be done if the company doesn't need their talents. It is a great question, and it is just as important as when the talents actually fit within the company. Yes, when we talk about talents "not fitting," we are really talking about firing someone. But even firing can be positive when handled with a GSP approach.

As an example, I'll tell you about Greg, one of the people I fired when I was general manager in Roanoke. Greg was having a devil of a time meeting performance expectations. He was a great guy, but he just couldn't get the results we wanted. After about six months of poor performance, he and I agreed to meet every other week to discuss his plan, progress, and lessons learned.

Every other Tuesday morning at 8:00 a.m. he and I got together in my office. At first we talked about his strengths and weaknesses, what he was good at, and what he just didn't like doing. We narrowed these down to a list of three each and put those on top of his performance improvement plan.

Then we talked about what we could do to leverage his strengths and minimize his weaknesses. We created a plan that accomplished both while aligning with the role he needed to do at our office. Since he was in sales, he would have to get better at some of his weak areas, like cold calling. He was not a man of initiative, so we decided to set weekly goals on how many customers he would call and how many he needed to visit.

Once we had that nailed down, the discussions turned to updates on his growth and behaviors. How many calls did he make? Did he attend the seminar we discussed? How many visits did he have? What did he learn from the sales calls? What deals were getting close? Every one of these meetings was bland at best. Greg didn't put in a lot of energy, and he seemed to have no real passion for being successful. He seemed to be just going through the motions. Then it occurred to me what the problem was.

Greg was a military guy. He grew up in the army and spoke fondly of it. During one of our meetings, he was updating me on a sales call he made on a customer who was from the military. His energy rose substantially as he described that guy and their conversation about the army. He actually got out of his chair when he described a formation exercise they both went through in boot camp. Then Greg sat down, and we both got real quiet. He looked at me and said, "What?"

"Greg, that was the most energy I have ever seen out of you. What just happened?" I asked. He sat there stunned for a moment and then said, "Yeah, I guess it was."

"How can we put you in a place where you have that energy much more often?" I asked. We discussed a few options, none of which was the real answer. Then I said, "Do you want to look back ten years from now and remember how you have felt for the last five years?"

His answer was rather quick: "No, I don't."

"Well then, let's make the tough decision today so that you can be in a much better spot tomorrow." He nodded, stood up, and walked toward my desk with his hand extended. That was the first time I had fired someone with a handshake.

Most firings end with a screaming match. My experience with Greg was a testament to the GSP belief. When we have the intent of helping people serve their purpose and be great, even the tough discussions are the right thing for them.

TOOLS

Talent Review

If you believe that associates want to be great and are the number-one priority for achieving business results, then you should be rigorous in your talent-review process. In fact, my experience indicates that the talent-review process should be one of the most important processes in a company.

The process is actually quite simple, although because we are talking about rating people, it must be done with clarity of intent and proper protocol. There are three goals to the process:

1. **Identify your best performers.** Make sure to keep your A players on your team and to provide the challenges they need to grow.

2. **Identify underperformers.** Per our belief that people want to GSP, no one wants to be mediocre C players. This process identifies C players and mandates a performance-improvement plan to move them to A- or B-level players within six months.

3. **Calibrate leadership ratings.** The collaboration within the leadership team helps you see and hear a broader view of your direct reports to make sure you have proper talent ratings by your leaders.

The process is not intended to automatically dispense of the bottom 10 percent. Instead, it is a process that is focused on doing the right thing for your associates. Your job as a leader is to help everyone succeed, on the premise that no one wants to perform poorly. This process holds leaders accountable by making sure that they are doing the right thing for their associates.

The process helps leaders rate every associate through predefined competencies and descriptions of A, B, and C ratings. In a traditional three-level organization (three levels of leadership), every leader rates direct reports with this tool and sends the tool to his or her manager. The manager then rates his or her direct reports and brings all of these ratings to the leadership team meeting.

At the end of the year, the leadership team meets to review every rating of every associate in the company. Although this sounds a bit overwhelming, it is actually not hard to accomplish because the focus of the discussions are on the A and C players. At the end of the meeting, a list of A and C players is developed and every leader is asked to create career plans for the A players and performance-improvement plans for the C players. HR is tasked with following up with the leaders to ensure this happens.

Hiring

This process guarantees that every hire has a great chance of being an A player. As described in the book *Topgrading: The Proven Hiring and Promoting Method that Turbocharges Company Performance* by Bradford Smart, an A player is the top 10 percent of the talent available for the role you are hiring for at the level of compensation you are willing to pay. If the hiring process consistently provides A players, then leaders have the confidence to replace C players who need to change roles. On the other hand, if the hiring process is inconsistent, it is less risky to keep existing players than to replace them.

Hiring is one of the most important responsibilities of a leader. If we get the right players and put them in the right positions, the company will drive itself. If we hire the wrong players, we are in a doom cycle that will cost tons of money, drop the culture, drive customer satisfaction lower, and result in poor business performance.

To make sure the hiring process is right, here are three key steps to follow:

1. **Identify core competencies for each role.** You must know what it takes to be successful in each role. Competencies can be broken down into talents, those things that we possess when we are born, and skills, those things that are developed over time. Energy is an example of a talent. Some people naturally have

high energy. On the other hand, project management is a skill. It is something learned through training and experience. For a project manager role, we would certainly look for project-management skills and skills around organization, yet just as importantly we would look for talents around composure, objectivity, and communication. For more information about talents, read the book *First, Break All the Rules: What the World's Greatest Managers Do Differently*.

2. **Create questions that identify talents.** It is easier to identify skills—we just need to probe into past experiences. Talents are another story. Because people are on their best behavior during interviews, we must be good at finding past behaviors that would indicate future behaviors. To do that, we must create questions that identify behaviors associated with talents rather than identifying the talents themselves. For instance, if we are looking for energy, we might ask, "When are you most productive?" or "What gets you down?" Make sure you have a clear list of questions that identify talents before going into an interview.

3. **Define the hiring-process steps.** Everyone must follow the prescribed process for hiring in your company. Following is a suggested format:

    a. **Complete a business pro forma of why the hire is important.** List cost, revenue growth, productivity, and any other factors that provide a business justification for the hire. Hiring leaders must first fill out this pro forma before requesting approval to hire.

    b. **Define culture questions to ensure culture fit.** In fact, 51 percent of the entire hiring decision should be based on culture fit.

c. **When approved by your superior or HR (if required), define the competencies required for this role and the questions you will use to find those competencies.**

d. **Create lists of associates and leaders who need to be involved in the process.** This should cover any role that works with this position, including any representatives from teams that work with this team.

e. **Post the role and conduct phone interviews to reduce the list of applicants.** Phone interviews should remove obvious non-fits but allow most applicants to proceed to the next step.

f. **Hold a panel interview to reduce the pool to the final three candidates.** Use the lists of associates and competency questions you've developed to rate each candidate and reduce to the pool to the top three candidates.

g. **Use a leadership interview to select the final candidate.**

h. **If there is a question about fit, do not hire.** Hiring slowly and cautiously is an absolute must. You would rather miss a good hire than hire a bad fit.

6

Belief: Enlightened Teams Achieve Superhuman Success

GSP PLUS CULTURE CLARITY EQUALS
HIGH-PERFORMANCE TEAMS

After being promoted to general manager, I figured out how I could take a world-class culture to the next level. The answer ended up being a personal-development process in which team leaders led each other to their individual purpose. We had taught each other the process to grow, serve, and perform (GSP).

Individual purpose was not the only lesson we learned from the personal-development class. We were all surprised by the sense of team spirit that we carried away from the class. The participants had learned both self-awareness and relationship awareness, and they began to see their peers' strengths and actively use these strengths to bolster the team's performance. They began to align the purpose of every individual on the team to create something much more powerful than just teamwork. This type of dynamic teaming process was something I had never experienced.

One of the leaders who attended the second personal-development class, David Smith, was just starting a new business within our company. The business concept was to solve a contracting problem for our customers. When it came to small HVAC-installation projects, our customers did not have many options, especially if they needed high-quality or engineering talents. It was going to be tricky to solve this problem because our company also sold equipment to contractors, and we did not want to compete with them or make them angry with us. In fact, it was so tricky that no other office had ever tried it. David and I thought it was worth a go, so we built our business plan to make it happen.

David had handpicked a core team of people based on their matching experiences, talents, and values with our defined business plan and company culture. He then used the personal-development class to help the team members discover their sense of individual purpose and develop the sense of teamwork needed for business success. He even included subcontracted labor in the personal-development class. During the class, he took the extra step of applying our company's vision, mission, and guiding principles to the work that his team would be doing. He was clear about how the team would make a difference and why that was important. He gave his team two key ingredients for success: GSP and culture clarity.

Culture clarity is providing a definition of the where, what, and how for any team or company. It is important that leaders and teams not allow culture to build without intention. By providing a clear definition of where we are going together (vision), what we do together (mission), and how we agree to behave together (guiding principles), leaders and team members have clarity on the culture they are trying to achieve and some accountability to live that culture.

The class taught his team about self-awareness and relationship awareness. Almost automatically, this awareness changed the behavior of his new team. They knew who would be great with customers and who would be great designing systems. Everyone felt they played an important role on a powerful team that was doing important work. They also understood what and why their team was important from the culture training around vision, mission, and guiding principles.

From the first customer response, it was clear that we were on to something. David's team was working on a hospital operating room, a very small but important job. The customer response to their performance on that project was huge. We got an email from the head nurse stating that it was the absolute best construction project she had ever experienced. She explained that the Trane people asked if the placement of their ladders was okay. "Every morning, the place looked like the construction project hadn't even started," she wrote. Then we got an email from the head of engineering, who commented on the excellence of the design and the quality of installation.

The business results quickly followed. We tripled the first-year business plan and doubled it in the second year. By year three, we were doing four times the business at above-average profit margins.

The class helped us form a new philosophy about teamwork. It also helped us build a new definition for performance. For me, it was an awakening. David's small team showed me what was possible—mixing GSP with culture clarity creates *enlightened teamwork*. By focusing on individual talents and then placing those individuals in a team where those talents can be used in concert, the value of the team explodes. David's group saw clearly how they needed each other to be a great team. This example also became a vision of something much more important. It was not difficult to see that high-performance teams can change a company, impact communities, and even change the world.

TEAMS GROW, SERVE, AND PERFORM TOO

The personal-development class made us aware of each individual's purpose through their strengths and talents. We then learned the second piece by applying each individual's purpose to the needs of the team (team awareness). Then David Smith added culture clarity to the personal-development class, and we saw all three together. And the three together equaled power.

There is something magical that can happen when a team achieves enlightenment. By "enlightenment," I mean becoming aware of yourselves, your teammates, and your culture. Three components of enlightened teams are

1. **Self-awareness:** Team members understand their individual strengths.

2. **Team awareness:** Team members understand the role they can play on the team and the talents of every other team member.

3. **Culture awareness:** Team members understand where the team is going, what the team does, and they agree how (using the guiding principles) to get the work done.

Teams in this state of enlightenment naturally flex their muscles in the right way for the right circumstance. If a customer calls with a technical problem, all team members will know the right technical teammate to serve the customer. If there is a complex problem within the business, they know which people on the team should get in a room to figure it out. All team members bring forward the right person or people, including themselves when appropriate, in the right situation. All team members feel important because they are respected for their strengths and get to use them often.

This concept applies to broader organizations as well. As discussed, as soon as someone becomes self-aware, he or she also becomes relationship-aware. When most of any organization's associates are self-aware, that organization already has two of the three magical ingredients to enlightened teamwork. They just need to add culture clarity to create the potion. If the organization adds a strong culture-development process to the personal-development class and the leadership team members behave as leaders, then the organization is only a few steps away from an enlightened organization.

The results for teams in this enlightened state are mind-boggling. David Smith's team achieved triple the first-year expectations and quadrupled the business in three years!

And it does work beyond smaller teams. My experience with the entire Virginia district team, which spans many offices and a large geography, proved this point. We deployed the class in all cities annually, which eventually lead to over 70 percent of the associates taking the class. It became a cornerstone of the district, as did the enlightenment it provided. And the results for the Virginia district were nothing short of excellence; they were the only offices in the country to exceed budget in three of the worst economic years!

A COMMUNITY COMES TOGETHER TO EDUCATE ITS CHILDREN

The fact that there are qualified high school graduates who cannot afford higher education is nothing new. Yet, when students have no hope for furthering their education, they generally drop out of high school altogether. If there were a program that helped us keep those students, powerful things could happen for everyone involved. For municipalities, the concept can mean converting a highly likely cost to society to a productive citizen. Such a program is also very interesting to school systems because it provides a reason for the poorest students to graduate high school, thus increasing graduation rates. It can also be powerful to businesses because they have a more highly qualified workforce to pull from.

With all the reasons to make such a program work, it is very rare in our country. The challenge is creating a program, funding it, and sustaining it among a community of diverse opinions and needs. As soon as politics get involved, the teamwork to achieve such a worthwhile cause is dismantled and the program never comes to fruition, except for one place in the blue ridge region of Virginia.

Roanoke's sister city, Salem, had started the program through the efforts of one man, Jerry Pace. Since Salem only had one high school and had limited need, an inventive man like Jerry made it all happen. When the same concept came to Roanoke, it failed to get traction multiple times. Either the sponsor wanted too much credit or the city felt neglected or the school system wanted more authority or so on and so on. In other words, people who focused on their individual needs got in the way of the greater good.

Finally, a team of people pulled the community together. First they identified the constituents from every corner of the community that needed to be involved. Then they brought all of these people together into one room and went through culture and self-awareness. More specifically, they showed everyone why they needed to create the program together and how it would positively impact the community and each attendee in the room. They set a vision and mission for the work this group of people would do. They put the why before the what.

Then they discussed the individual talents in the room. From business and city council to superintendent and marketing and communications, every member of the team was important and valuable. There were over twenty-five people in the room that day, yet every person had a role to play in achieving the vision. That meeting was pivotal. It set culture and self-awareness in place, which allowed leadership and action to play its role.

This team of leaders representing all aspects of the community came together to achieve something incredible. They built a funding mechanism that had public and private entities sharing the load. They created sustaining mechanisms to ensure the funding would continue through defined joint agreements and steering committees. They worked with the local community college to set up curriculum and support processes to help the kids learn valuable skills, which would eventually serve the needs within the community and the local businesses. This team became an enlightened team and achieved superhuman results.

The blue ridge region is now one of only a handful of places in North America that has created their own community college access program (CCAP) where all high school graduates can go to college if their grades meet the minimums and if they are unable to afford the tuition.

TOOLS

Becoming an enlightened organization is a great goal to have, but it takes hard work to achieve. Following is the entire personal-development process—applicable to all associates on your team or organization—to develop the self-awareness required to create enlightened teams.

At the end of the book, you will see how all these beliefs come together into a system. Within the system are foundational beliefs, structural beliefs, and ultimate beliefs. Foundational beliefs define the cultural norms that must exist for teamwork and individual growth to flourish. Structural beliefs provide clarity on how to develop associates, leaders, and the culture. Ultimate beliefs connect teamwork and culture to high-performing business results and they sustain the culture and the high-performing results. Each of these beliefs builds upon the others to form a systemic approach to business leadership. (See figure 6.1.)

We will get into more detail about the foundational and ultimate beliefs soon enough. For now, let's focus on the structural beliefs that build our ultimate belief that enlightened teams achieve superhuman success.

Personal-Development Plans

The personal-development course we created in Roanoke helped all the participants develop self-awareness, relationship awareness, and strong teamwork. It is important to know that there were no professional trainers or facilitators in the original class or any classes since. Here's the process we follow:

Step 1: Pick your team. First you must pick your students of leadership. These people can be anyone in the company, but they should be interested in personal or leadership development.

Step 2: Set your price of admission. All students must commit to the course. They must also be willing to do homework. Reading books or attending courses is generally the two preferred admission tickets.

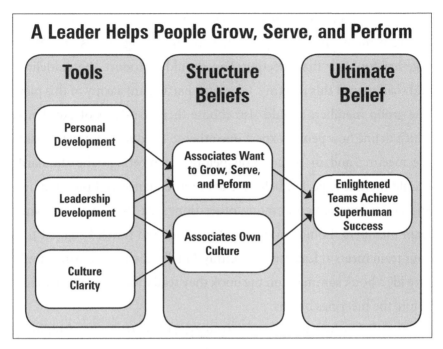

Figure 6.1: Systemic Approach to Business Leadership

Good choices are books like

- *Good to Great: Why Some Companies Make the Leap . . . and Others Don't* by Jim Collins
- *Practice What You Preach: What Managers Must Do to Create a High Achievement Culture* by David Maister
- *We Shall Not Fail: The Inspiring Leadership of Winston Churchill* by Celia Sandys and Jonathan Littman
- *First, Break All the Rules: What the World's Greatest Managers Do Differently* by Marcus Buckingham and Curt Coffman

Make sure that at most three people read the same book, so that a diverse set of perspectives is acquired from the reading assignment.

Step 3: Hold your first meeting. After providing enough time for the team members to complete their reading assignments, pull them together for their first meeting. You should introduce the guidelines and road map at this meeting. Give each participant a copy of this plan. The group members should also choose their standards of excellence, which define how people expect one other to conduct themselves inside the meeting and in preparation before the meeting. The standards should include expected behavior about attendance, cell phone usage, and active involvement, among other things. At the same time, your team members should choose meeting dates and times. I suggest that your team meets at least twice monthly. Finally, each participant should provide a book summary on the book they read to all other participants before the meetings begins.

Step 4: Use an open-forum strategy. This is the start of building synergy among the teammates. Use this time to discuss leadership in any form or fashion. The idea is to get people talking and thinking about leadership. Use the ideas generated from the reading assignments to get the participants rolling. Let the discussion go anywhere it takes you as long as it is about leadership. The homework assignment for the group is to think about the top ten characteristics of a leader.

Step 5: Choose your top ten. The next one or two meetings should be used to discuss the top ten characteristics of great leaders. At the end of these meetings, the group members should have a consensus on their top ten. The homework assignment after the consensus has been reached is for all members to do a self-assessment by rating themselves from 1 to 10 on each characteristic. Each team member should also do an assessment of all other team members.

Step 6: Ask yourself: Who am I? Participants should offer their self-assessment to the group for open discussion. The feedback should be direct with respect. People should openly discuss their self-assessment and then listen as the other team members provide their assessment of them. This bluntly honest discussion is critical to the success of all members, because without feedback they cannot modify their styles. Two other outcomes happen because of this feedback. First, the team builds a special bond that will last beyond the leadership training. Second, each member of the team learns how to be direct with respect, which is a powerful culture builder. Homework for this step is to read *People Styles at Work and Beyond: Making Bad Relationships Good and Good Relationships Better* by Robert Bolton and Dorothy Grover Bolton. This should be read within the next three meetings for a discussion at the third meeting.

Step 7: Ask others: What do you think? The next assignment is for all participants to ask five other associates in the company *outside* the group to rate them 1 to 10, using the same feedback criteria they used among the group. The feedback should be summarized and discussed in the next meeting. The follow-up homework is for participants to pick some of the best and worst ratings or comments and have a face-to-face discussion with the associate who made that observation. Again, this should be thrown on the table for all. The homework for this step is to issue the social-style questionnaire that is located in the *People Styles at Work* book to at least five associates.

Step 8: Ask yourself: Who am I? Part II. Begin the meeting with an open exchange on the social styles that were learned from the book and how people with those styles react with people of the others. Discussions about flexibility and mentoring should also be included. During the class, the group should chart each other's styles from the questionnaire. Homework for this step is to pick the social style of at least three people you manage or work with and decide how you should modify your style to communicate better with them. The discussion in the next class asks all participants to determine their style and how they can modify their styles to best provide leadership and mentoring.

Step 9: Create your plan. All individuals compile what they have learned about themselves into one summary and develop the prioritized list of issues on which to focus. Brainstorm with the group for ideas on receiving the proper training, experience, and feedback necessary for improvement. Each member should then pick the one item they are going to develop for personal growth. Each member should also pick a sponsor. The sponsor is someone who works with the individual often and is willing to give direct feedback on an ongoing basis about that single development item.

Step 10: Commit to ongoing improvement. The meetings should move to once a quarter at this stage. This is simply the ongoing growth portion, but it is no less critical. Review plans at least once quarterly and ascertain a subjective way of measuring success.

Interestingly enough, this process can be used for anyone looking to grow. Even if you are trying to increase your success in a nonleadership role, you can use this process to determine your strengths and weaknesses. Once again, the goal is to help people become great. The process is the same.

7

Belief: Purposeful Associates Create Loyal Customers Who Maximize Business Results (the ACBs)

AN ENLIGHTENED TEAM TEACHES ANOTHER LESSON

The lessons I learned from my time in the Roanoke Trane office by being around the amazing associates and culture were finally all coming together. Learning how to create superteams convinced me that the sky was the limit; we could do anything once we learned self-awareness and culture clarity. But the greatest lesson was yet to come.

As discussed in the last chapter, David Smith had created an incredible contracting business from scratch by combining the lessons from the personal-development class with the idea and practice of culture clarity. I sat down with David to review his progress and asked him what he attributed his success to. His answer was straightforward: "We have a great team of people who serve customers much better than any other option the customer has to choose from. Once we serve a customer the first time, they are ours for life."

David and I discussed how he began the process by putting the right people on the team. He selected them by matching their talents with what he needed the team to accomplish *and* by their fit to the culture he needed them to work within. Then he used the personal-development class to build self-awareness in his people, who also understood the talents of each other. And, maybe most important, David conveyed to the team why their work was important by connecting them to a strong vision and mission. He taught them about the culture we were trying to create by providing culture clarity.

David confirmed the lessons I had recently learned about how a leader does not need to be a hammer and about how—by building an enlightened team—we could work together in new and better ways toward a common vision. But David had also taken an extra step. He had connected all of these thoughts into a continuum that led very clearly to positive business results. The lesson I learned from David's team was that culture clarity—when combined with associates and customers, the two most important components of business success—was essential for high-performance results.

Concurrent with starting the small contracting business (David's team), we were starting a very large contracting business. It cost a lot of money to get this business off the ground, which meant if we didn't sell something quickly, we would be in trouble financially. If there were ever a perfect test for the culture process and its connection to business results, this was it.

This business relied on partners to do the installation work rather than Trane's team. The biggest trick of this business was its size. We were selling very large projects, sometimes over $10 million each, that were based on energy savings that would pay for the cost of the project over time. It was very difficult to sell this work because each project had multiple buyers and each of the buyers had to get approval before purchasing. Many districts before us had failed in this business.

There were also many people involved in the selling process. The team included salespeople, energy engineers, project developers, and estimators. To get the work done would require project managers, measurement specialists, superintendents, and specially trained technicians. The number of people involved made the selling process complex; no wonder failure was more likely than success.

But the proof was in the process and the profits. Our culture and our new beliefs built the foundation for the success of this new contracting business. Following David's model for the small contracting team, we selected people based on their experience in this business and for the culture we needed them to work within. Team members who had not been through the personal-development class went through it. The leadership of the group provided culture clarity for this team around the vision, mission, and guiding principles.

Once again, the business results went through the roof. Within two years, the Roanoke office had the largest contracting business in North America. That year marked the first in five consecutive years of the Virginia district winning the contracting office of the year. This was an unparalleled dynasty of success at Trane.

As I looked back on these two business successes, David's words rang in my head: "We have a great team of people who serve customers much better than any other option they have to choose from. Once we serve a customer, they are ours for life."

As I thought about it more and more, the process could be boiled down to three elements: associates, customers, and business. We had figured out how to build great people and great teams and passionately serve customers with those people and teams, a process that, in turn, delivered strong business results. It is the connection and sequence of these three that formed the conviction for my next roles within our company. I was convinced that this was the route to success in any organization. In fact, I knew it was the route to success in just about any situation or setting.

Looking back, I can see that my years as a general manager were life changing for me. Leadership became synonymous with world-changing purpose. I felt obligated to search all of my associates for their strengths while guiding them to become the best they could be through service. Most importantly, I was proof that this new philosophy on culture and leadership could be learned and taught. I felt a calling to teach this advanced form of leadership to everyone in our company because the only way to build enlightened teamwork was to build enlightened leaders.

As more and more Roanoke associates became self-aware and relationship-aware of their individual strengths, the new definition of leadership and teamwork was displayed in real time; we provided world-class service to customers, and the customers responded with a wealth of profitable business. It became clear that we were all talented. A natural respect for each other took place, and a natural placement of each talent in the right spot through candid discussions became common. The team decided who would join them and removed those who did not fit.

I summarized what I had learned as *purposeful associates create loyal customers who maximize business results*, or the "ACBs."

MY STRUGGLES AT HOME

Although I was learning a lot at work about the ACBs and leadership in general, I was not learning a lot about how to be a better leader at home or a husband and father, for that matter. My success at work was not following me home, and it was clear to me that this incongruence should not exist. How could and should I bring the life lessons from work into my whole life?

With all the time I spent on the two new and challenging jobs in three years, I fell out of balance with my family. I had a fabulous wife and three beautiful children, but they were no longer my first priority. Some might say they weren't even my second priority. At that point, the kids were five, seven, and ten. And though I realized that it was a very busy time for the family and that I was needed as a father and a husband, when I got home I was beat and not really there. My mind was on the challenges I had faced at work or what I needed to do the next day. Shelby would be worn out from being the sole family leader all day, and she would need a break when I got home, which I rarely gave her.

I remember one time watching my son talk to his sisters with a lack of patience and disrespect that I had shown him. I was watching my own behavior in my son, and it hit me like a ton of bricks. I sat down in shame. It was clear something had to change in my life, and, even though Shelby was gracious enough to oblige for the time being, I had to figure it out soon.

ACBs—ASSOCIATES, CUSTOMERS, AND BUSINESS RESULTS

It is obvious that the customer who writes the check is important to a company's profits. This means that customers are directly connected to business results. They evaluate, decide, buy, and provide feedback on products and services. If they like what they see, are happy with its price, think it adds value to what they are trying to accomplish, find it is easy and inexpensive to operate, and think it is better than the competition's product, then you would have a darn good business model.

But customers are not the leader's first priority. The reason is straightforward: most leaders do not serve customers; associates do. Your associates are in contact with your customers. Are your associates happy? Are they serving? Are they adding value? The answers to these questions will decide what your company looks like to your customers.

This is not only true for customer-facing associates. The associates who make the products decide the quality of the products. They also decide the level of productivity in getting the product produced and, therefore, the cost of the product.

Remember, it is called the "ACBs" of business leadership. Purposeful associates (As) create loyal customers (Cs) who generate premier business performance (Bs). The priorities, sequence, and consistency are all important. I suggest you commit these points to memory:

1. All business decisions should consider the impact on the ACBs.

2. The sequence of priority is associates, then customers, and then business.

3. Business reviews should balance metrics for the ACBs.

When I say that business decisions must consider the impact on the ACBs, I mean that every major decision should include a discussion about the impact the decision will have on your associates, customers, and business. If business leaders stringently follow the ACBs and ask the ACB questions with every important decision, the ACB thought process will flow through the organization. It will become the overarching definition of the culture. Decisions will be balanced and people will feel important.

As discussed, you must also sequence or prioritize: the As come before the Cs, which come before the Bs. Maintaining this sequence is often the toughest part to execute in real life. The higher you get in management, the closer you are to the financials and the further you move from customers and associates. As a leader of leaders, I now see associates much less, and I rarely see customers. On the other hand, I get emails and phone calls about the financials almost daily.

Although the ACBs are the right approach, the pressure on managers can actually come in reverse: BCA. Once you get to a certain level of management, 90 percent of the questions coming from your superior will be about the financials. This singular focus inevitably forces the majority of a leader's time to the B rather than the A. The same pressure flows downhill quickly if you are not careful.

This brings us to the third point covered earlier. Business reviews should balance the metrics for associates, customers, and business. If you can balance the pressure on business results with equal pressure on associate engagement and customer loyalty, then you ensure that the right decisions and cultural messages are being sent from the top.

The core obstacle to continuous ACB balance is metrics. It is easy to find metrics to measure your business. It is much more difficult to find metrics to measure your associates and customers. The ACBs ask that you take the time to find meaningful data on your associates and customers. This means adding qualitative information to your quantitative decision making and using it.

The ACB approach is a system of beliefs that are organic in nature. Customer satisfaction does drive business results, yet associate engagement is the number-one determinant of customer satisfaction. If business leaders allow the ACBs to happen, the teams below them will naturally lead the ACBs.

CARING ASSOCIATES CREATE LOYAL CUSTOMERS

Why are people loyal? Think about the places where you have put your loyalty in the past. Then think about why you put it there. When you boil it down, your customers become loyal based on their answers to these three questions:

1. Are you trustworthy?

2. Do you care about me?

3. Are you committed to excellence?

Remember, trust depends on both character and competency. The first question focuses on character. Essentially, it asks whether you do the right thing for your customers. If your customers are confident that you are trustworthy, they will buy from you again. If not, they will find someone they can trust to purchase from in the future.

The first question only opens the door. Customers' answers to the next two questions about you determine whether they will be loyal. "Do you care about me?" takes over where the trust question left off. If a customer perceives that he can trust your company, he needs to know if you really care about him. This question is really asking, "Am I important to you?" Loyalty begins with how you treat others. If you treat your customers with importance and caring, they will tend to care about you and begin to become loyal.

The answer to third question—"Are you committed to excellence?"—tells the customer whether you will execute or not. Will you get the job done, and will it be a high-quality job?

Another way to look at the question of "Why do customers *give* their loyalty?" is to ask, "Why do customers *take away* their loyalty?"

The American Society of Quality Control studied why customers leave businesses and found the following:

1. Customer was turned away by the indifferent attitude of employee (68 percent).

2. Customer was dissatisfied with the product (14 percent).

3. Customer was lured away by competition (9 percent).

4. Customer was influenced by a friend to go elsewhere (5 percent).

5. Customer moved away (3 percent).

6. Death of the customer (1 percent).

The majority, 68 percent, left because they did not feel the business associates cared about them or because they did not think the business was committed to excellence.[2] Once customers come in the door, they decide to return based on how they are treated. The associate decides to act in a way that fosters trust, to treat the customer with respect and caring, and to provide excellent service and results. Your customers may walk through the door because of your brand, but they will decide to stay because of your people.

TOOLS

There are processes that ensure we are taking care of associates, serving customers, and achieving as a business. These core processes cover strategy, planning, execution, and everything in between. If we clearly define those processes and set them in place to happen consistently, we are more likely to get them done in an excellent way.

---

2. Roger Fritz, "The Top Reasons Customers Leave," *San Francisco Business Times*, October 19, 1997.

Business Operating System

In the appendix, there is an example of the business operating system (BOS) tool. This tool helps leaders create an overall plan for executing the ACBs of leadership. The BOS not only combines all of the ACB processes, it also puts them into a calendar framework to ensure certain steps are taken each month. Leadership teams review the BOS once a month to remind them what is due that month and what they need to prepare for next month.

These are the major ideas broken into three categories: core processes, one-time events, and annual processes.

Core Processes

1. Hiring
2. Culture development

One-Time Events

1. ACB posters
2. Culture cards

Annual Processes

1. Talent review
2. Feedback
3. Training
4. Culture (reviews, new associate measurement)
5. Planning
6. Budget

7. Goal-setting (scorecards)

8. Monthly operations reviews

9. Strategy

10. Fix-it events

8

Belief: Excellence is Driven from the Ground Up

THE BEST LEADERSHIP IDEAS COME FROM PEOPLE YOU LEAD

I thought my transformation from individual contributor to leader was complete. But there was more to learn (there always is). As a general sales manager, I learned that the associates own the culture and leaders must lead. The general manager role taught me that people want to grow, serve, and perform. It also taught me about enlightened teams and the ACBs. But now it was time to use these core beliefs to create a vibrant culture from the ground up.

While I was general sales manager in Roanoke, Jeff Watson was asked to be the first territory vice president for Trane North America. Felix Wilson replaced Jeff as the Virginia district manager. Where Jeff taught me about Jess and culture, Felix taught me about business leadership. He was a business and financial genius (yes, another huge blessing for my career). He also promoted me to general manager. About three years into Felix's tenure in Virginia, something very interesting happened. The leader of the largest Trane district, Dallas, was removed from his position and Felix's name was one of the first to be mentioned as his potential replacement.

I was on the road when my cell phone buzzed. It was Jeff Watson, who had the power to decide who would replace Felix as district manager for Virginia Trane. (If you are counting blessings for me, we have now hit double digits!) He got to the point quickly: "Jason, congrats bud, you are now the district manager of Virginia."

I pulled off the road into a parking lot. *Amazing*, I thought. I immediately remembered the goal I set back in my initial years with Trane in Lacrosse. After hearing about the district manager role, I realized I'd met my goal of being a district manager by the time I was thirty-nine. At thirty-eight, I had actually beaten that goal by a year, and I had no idea how. *I am so darn blessed* I thought, and then I put my head down and started thanking God for my many blessings. I remember it being so very clear that He was guiding my path. My commitment from that day forward, although I screwed this one up as often as any of the others, was to find and fulfill His purpose, and I was confident that He had a grand plan for me.

After the official announcement, I put together a ninety-day plan for getting up to speed on the Virginia district. I was armed with new beliefs about individuals, teams, and cultures. I strongly believed in the ACBs and looked forward to leading them for a larger team. Knowing it was all about the people, I wanted to spend face-to-face time with every associate in Richmond. I wanted to build relationships with everyone on my new leadership team, because I knew that leadership was a leverage point. Throughout the first ninety days, I made notes about every meeting, and afterward I looked back on those notes. It was clear that Felix and Jeff had done a great job putting the right people in the right places. Some of the leaders and associates were questionable, but not many. I put in place plans to evaluate the questionable people and move them to the right spots rather quickly, so we could get to the main goal of building a high-performing culture.

Then it was time to work on self-awareness, GSP, and building enlightened teams. I was confident about how to make that happen. We picked the influential associates of Richmond and started their first personal-development class. Whereas Roanoke had a long history of strong culture and leadership, Richmond had the exact opposite. Like the classes in Roanoke, the students in Richmond were engaged from moment one, and they seemed even thirstier for this discussion than the Roanoke students. It was like they had unconsciously needed this type of interaction and it had been missing for a long time. While Roanoke associates were willing to guard the culture they created, Richmond associates were determined to build the culture that was possible. Since we sped up the class, within six months about 20 percent of the associates in the Richmond office had experienced self-awareness and were becoming relationship-aware as well. These associates were able to lead the other 80 percent rather quickly.

Within the first thirty days, I took the Richmond service manager, Mike Martin, to dinner. I could tell he was neither happy nor effective where he was, yet I could also tell he was someone we needed on our team. He had our culture and was committed to our company. He had even been successful in previous roles. During the dinner, we discussed his talents and his past experiences in which his talents had made a real difference. He spoke of feeling "passionate and excited" in the past. I asked him if he still had that passion and excitement. His answer was candid and took lots of courage: "No, Jason, I do not." "Well then," I said, "let's get you into a role where you can get that excitement back again."

Mike agreed to take a step back so that he could take a step forward in the future. I demoted Mike to project manager, and he began rebuilding his leadership capabilities for the next leadership opportunity. He attended the personal-development class and became one of the passionate 20 percent. Mike confirmed what I had learned in Roanoke: everyone wants to grow, serve, and perform, and my job as a leader was to facilitate this process. But I soon realized that once the culture has been implanted, the associates facilitate it as well.

Not long after the first class, one of the star students, Diane Martin, who was a project manager in our equipment business, came to me with a request. "Jason, this class is changing who we are and I don't want it to stop. Have you ever considered a level-two personal-development class?" I told her that I would think about it. Her question stuck with me for two reasons. First was the challenge to find the next phase of personal development. The second was that she wanted more. She had a desire to build what was possible. She was owning the culture development.

Concurrent with the personal-development classes, I was traveling to the four offices that made up the Richmond area, spreading the word and ensuring we had the right leaders in place. Every office received a culture review from me, and then, six months later, they received a culture mid-year review. The cool thing was that everyone was excited to have the discussion. There was no need to try to convince them. In fact, it was the exact opposite. It was almost as if they were asking, "What took you management people so long?" Their natural desire for the ACBs created quick and strong momentum.

EXCELLENCE IS DRIVEN FROM THE GROUND UP

Change is not easy. Routines and habits guide our lives. To suddenly change a routine is disruptive at best and highly stressful most of the time.

Change curves start with "bad stuff" for a reason. Humans don't generally like change. We go through many initial phases, anger and denial among them, before we start to test and adopt change.

It is also true that often we are too close to something to see that change is needed. If we are in the middle of a process, we can see our little piece of that process, but it is tough to see the whole process. It is even tougher to see how a completely new system could improve the lives, efficiency, and effectiveness of everyone, especially if it makes our little portion of the system worse for us or makes it disappear.

For these reasons, change is generally driven from the top down. Leaders have the best understanding of the situation from a holistic perspective. They certainly need representation from those within the system to understand what is really happening and what needs to be considered when changing the system, but leaders must take responsibility for the tough change decisions. They must also take ownership of helping their associates get through the change curve as quickly as possible.

Leaders generally lead change from the top down, but leaders should not expect excellence from the change. In fact, as a leader you should expect your associates to create excellence. Excellence applies to everything that happens within your systems and processes, everything you do to serve customers. Where do you waste time? Where do you spend unneeded effort? How could you make the process better, quicker, easier? Think of it as the amount of work it takes to get an order and turn it into cash.

If we charted every action it takes with our current process, we might find a very extensive map with many people, steps, systems, and paths to get from here to there. If we then asked our associates to fix the process by reducing steps and increasing efficiency, we might see amazing results. Pretty quickly the people doing the work would realize that if they could find ways to improve the process, they could make their jobs easier. As they change their thinking, they start to recognize the many frustrations that exist in getting their jobs done.

I have personally witnessed this from the ground up. I have seen it implemented in places as varied as manufacturing plants and sales offices. Often businesses are able to reduce time and energy more than 50 percent. The time and energy saved is just half of what they find. They also find higher associate engagement because the associates are able to spend more time adding value instead of spending time on steps that don't add value. As discussed in previous chapters, increased engagement drives business results.

THERE HAS TO BE A CULTURE CONSCIOUSNESS

About six months into my tenure at Richmond, Diane came into my office with Matte Anderson. Matte was the sales leader in Richmond, and he was by far the wisest leader I had ever met. Diane was the kind of lady who showed up just when you needed her to, whether you knew it or not, and she always seemed to say just what you needed to hear. This time was no exception. "Jason," Diane said, "you have done a great job taking our culture to the next level. It feels great around here." Matte nodded and gave me a little wink. "The problem is that *you* still own the culture. It needs to be owned by *us*. There has to be a culture consciousness. How do we do that?" Matte smiled, but I was a little confused.

Culture consciousness?! Those are some powerful words, I thought. Of course, Diane was reminding me of the lesson I had learned in my past role—associates own the culture. What she reminded me of was the time when Jeff Watson, my dad, and I were in my living room talking about management and leadership. Jeff asked my dad, formerly a high-level business leader for IBM, "How did you lead?" My dad's answer was simple: "I put teams of people together without leaders to solve our greatest problems."

Diane was saying what my dad had said: associates own the culture, but they need to own the culture development too, so that they can fix our major problems.

Over the next month, Matte led Diane and me into several discussions about culture consciousness. He told us about how we all, associates and leaders, naturally want to serve our individual purpose and be a part of a team that is doing something special. When we put it into business words that I could understand, I realized he was saying that individuals want to grow, serve, and perform, and teams naturally want to live the ACBs. People want to be great. When a business allows them to do that, they are energized and functioning from their core values. He also said that people wanted to be on enlightened teams and that teams wanted to be great too. Looking back on my first six months in Richmond, he was exactly right. The teams wanted to go there. They were wondering what took our company so long to allow it.

We soon came to two conclusions. First, we realized that, to hone Diane's point, the culture development must be owned by the associates and not the leaders. To do this, we needed to select a team of associates—not leaders—who would lead all the other associates in Richmond toward culture ownership. They would serve as our culture team. This team would define where our culture needed to go and the actions we would take to get there. Since associates would lead the team, there would be a natural buy in and speed to action with the rest of the organization.

Second, we needed to prepare the members of the culture team for their work. If they were going to effectively lead other associates on the complex subject of culture, they would need training on core leadership subjects such as culture, change management, building trust, and communications. As you might have guessed, Diane's original idea about a "level-two personal-development class" was the training our culture team would need to lead our entire company on culture. Similar to Personal Development I, the pilot for Personal Development II, as we now called the two classes, could be used throughout the company afterward.

Within two months, we began the pilot program. It was both a great start to the culture team and a powerful statement about the culture of Richmond. Not only were they getting it, they were also *leading it* for all of Virginia. They, like their Roanoke peers years before them, soaked up the training, and, with the goal of cultural development, they made every class better with their ownership. When they completed the class, Personal Development II was ready for deployment across the district, and the culture team was ready to develop the culture in Richmond and the Virginia district.

CULTURE CONSCIOUSNESS ENCOURAGES ASSOCIATES TO CO-CREATE STRATEGY

With the core training behind them, I held a few meetings with the team to build our charter and define our goals. We spent plenty of time talking about culture in general and specifically what we wanted our culture to be in the future. They then went to work building and executing the plan.

The culture committee first suggested we create a culture team of associates in Roanoke to work in conjunction with the culture team in Richmond. They realized that the culture consciousness was for Virginia Trane, not just for Richmond. These two teams then created what was soon to be known as "The Virginia Way," which was shortened to "VaWay." VaWay put the future in present tense and defined what our culture was and what it was going to be. It was a communication and action plan for developing the culture we wanted to have in the Virginia district. It said, "We are great today, but we are taking steps now to be even better tomorrow." The message implied that Virginia could lead the culture of the entire Trane company. They believed they could change the world.

The VaWay was soon telling *me* what to do. From providing me with core messages to include in my communications to coming up with the theme for our annual meeting, the VaWay team was leading our company's culture to the next level. They defined what was great about us in straightforward language, and they got specific about what must be added to our culture to make it better. They picked three behaviors that needed focus: associate learning, creating, and deciding. They told all associates that they needed to learn something new every day, that they needed to create better ways to serve customers, and that they were now empowered to make decisions to serve each other and our customers.

Thank goodness that the culture committee had taken control, because Shelby's patience with me had run its course. I remember sitting in O'Charley's, a bar in Richmond, about to order dinner, when Shelby called. I can even remember the exact booth I was sitting in because I had been there for two hours. (Don't worry, I tipped well). Shelby was done. She was not happy with our life and not happy with the role I was playing as a father or a husband. I told her I would drive home immediately, but she said, "No, let's talk now."

This was it. I had to change my personal life like I had changed my business life. I made the switch right then from slightly involved husband to completely committed life partner. I remember telling myself that I was going to take 100 percent responsibility for my relationship with my wife and that I would not pin any of it on her. The 100%–0% concept was still fresh in my mind. After two hours of explaining to Shelby that I realized I had not been who I should have been and that I would change from that moment forward, she believed me. Thank God!

Back at work, the VaWay was alive and well. We created a message that articulated where we were going with our culture and the role each associate had to play to get us there. We wanted everyone to think about *how* they did their jobs and how they created and made decisions. They, more than anyone, knew how their jobs worked and how their jobs could be done better.

To address the how, we created a program called the "Fix-It" event. We pulled a cross-functional team of associates, representing all sub-teams in the company, into a two-day meeting. Before the meeting, they were asked to get their sub-teams' feedback on things that needed fixing. During the two days, the Fix-It team listed these suggestions on a board and, as a team, reduced the list to the top items. From there, they broke into teams to build small business plans for each of the top items. The climax of the two-day meeting was when I stood at the front of the room and listened to associates present business plans one by one. I had to approve or deny the business plans on the spot. If I approved, the presenter was named "virtual boss" and was empowered to go fix the problem with his or her plan.

The results were dramatic. People saw that they could create new and innovative ways to serve each other and customers better. They also saw that they were empowered to make decisions. Those who attended the first Fix It event were so excited that they spread the word across the company, which made the other associates feel empowered as well. Similar to how we helped associates find self-awareness and then connect that awareness to team purpose through the personal-development class, the VaWay was leading our culture development by describing what was going to change and then helping all associates live the new behavior in real time.

A few years into VaWay, Virginia and three other districts piloted a culture-development process for all of Trane. The first step was to measure our existing culture with a tool called the Denison Culture Survey. The survey was unique not just because it measured culture, but also because it allowed for slicing and dicing of culture metrics for each office in a district as well as each leader in a leadership team. When the results came back for all four pilot offices, there was no doubt which culture was the leader. Virginia had one of the highest culture scores Denison had ever seen. And, most impressively, both Richmond and Roanoke had similar scores. The VaWay had made a great culture better and a poor culture great. It had also started influencing the entire company.

The total Virginia district soon took home company awards and an increase in business profit. By the time I had left the Virginia district for my next role, Virginia Trane had won the service office of the year, the top office of the year, and the contracting office of the year four times. Even better, Virginia Trane was the only office to exceed financial expectations in three of the most economic challenging years ever. Of particular note were the dramatic results in Richmond. Their market share grew over 20 percent. Their contracting business grew over 100 percent. Their service and parts business grew substantially as well.

Things were changing back at home too. I dropped my excuse that I was tired. I no longer allowed myself to be short or impatient. I also dropped my tendency to focus on Shelby's faults. Just like at work, I began looking for the strengths—and she had many. She felt the change, and the culture of our home changed too. The conflict between the work Jason and the home Jason was now resolved and I was a much better leader for it.

The ability to take the skills I learned in Roanoke to a green field in Richmond was exactly the practice I needed as a leader. With my new beliefs firmly implanted in my brain, Richmond became a testing ground to master these new skills. People *did* want to grow, serve, and perform. Enlightened teams *do* achieve superhuman success. And purposeful associates *do* create loyal customers who *do* maximize business results. I certainly made my mistakes, but there were also many successes and real-life lessons in the game of culture leadership.

Richmond also gave me a new gift: by watching the culture teams and the Fix-It event they created, I became a firm believer that excellence happens when those who are doing the work think about how to make it better, rather than focusing on what they need to do next. When people feel empowered to work on the *how*, not just the *what*, the impact is excellence and an energized and engaged workforce.

It was clear to me that the culture-building process I had learned in Roanoke could be deployed anywhere. Roanoke taught me how to lead the process and now I could teach others. I also learned a valuable lesson about becoming a total leader. Leadership wasn't just at work. It was in every aspect of my life, from my work and family to my spirituality and community.

LARRY'S TEAM GETS TO THE MARKET FAST

Senior leaders asked Larry, the North American leader of product engineering, to bring new products to the market in less than half the time of past results. The company's products were trailing the competition, and market share was falling. New products were needed as soon as possible.

Larry's first step was to bring the team together and discuss the challenge, to deliver high-value, high-quality products in half the time. In fact, since the first meeting, senior leaders had gotten more specific. They wanted a new product in six months rather than two years. After the initial gasp, the team members jumped in with both feet. They detailed the engineering process, including how it connects to the production process. They found multiple ways to reduce the process and increase the speed without having an impact on quality. They made a list of key changes that needed to be reviewed by senior leaders, including approval processes and investment dollars.

Larry, together with key team members, presented the new process for the required senior leader decisions. All were approved for immediate implementation. The team was fired up. They had found a way to decrease the time of the process by 75 percent and had full support from senior leaders for their efforts. Long story short, the end result was the first product delivered within six months!

"FIX-IT" IS MUCH MORE THAN PROBLEM SOLVING

As the Fix-It process matures and, more importantly, the process becomes a part of the company's culture, associates within the organization begin finding ways to improve all processes. Instead of relying on a group meeting to find improvement ideas, they find them and fix them on the fly. From the original event, the associates feel empowered to find and fix when necessary. It becomes a culture of continuous improvement.

This is what is meant by excellence being driven from the ground up. It is a win-win approach that achieves the magical combination of increased productivity and increased associate engagement—all with the leader serving as coach rather than director. Not a bad way to achieve business success, is it?

The power of implementing their ideas certainly drove productivity. In fact, after they initiated the Fix-It program, the Virginia district exceeded average company productivity every year. However, the power of this meeting was much more than the productivity results. When the attendees returned to their teams, they told them about what happened. They became the personal advocate for the culture of finding and fixing on the fly.

Those empowered associates drove a new culture that made fixing on the fly a norm. And it was the fix on the fly that drove the engagement scores of the Virginia district through the roof. In fact, the Virginia district achieved one of the highest engagement scores in the nation to go with one of the highest business growth rates. These strong business results were driven by best-in-class associate engagement.

TOOLS

Fix-It Event

As you have learned, the Fix-It event can have a powerful outcome for your associates and your company. The great news is that it is relatively easy to host the meeting:

1. **Schedule milestones.** Figure 8.1 lists the milestones of a Fix-It event.

2. **Select a local champion for the Fix-It forum.** The champion will be responsible for the following items:

   - Determine role and responsibilities. Decide who will help the champion make the meeting happen.
   - Organize and plan. Take ownership of the plan and execution.
   - Facilitate the event.
   - Communicate the outcomes.

3. **Introduce the program to all associates.** The purpose of the presentation is to provide a high-level overview of the journey to all associates and to define the overall purpose of the initiative. Discuss that the local leadership has buy in to the Fix-It forum, and that the local champion has been chosen. Consider

Fix-It Milestone	Timing (# weeks prior to event)
Leader develops understanding of process	4–8
Select champion	4–8
Introduce the forum to all associates	4–6
Establish logistics for the event	2–4
Select associates ("product managers") to participate in the event; conduct call with selected associates	2–3
Program managers request Fix-It ideas from their assigned associates	2–3
Program managers compile Fix-It ideas submitted by their assigned associates	1
Conduct Fix-It forum	Day of Event

Figure 8.1: Fix-It Steps

showing the following *Saturday Night Live* skit regarding Fix-It, which may add some perspective to the forum and certainly adds some fun: "Update with Oscar Rogers: 'Fix It.'"

4. **Cover the associates' roles and responsibilities for a Fix-It forum.** These may include generating ideas, possibly participating in the forum, and helping implement those ideas.

5. **Establish the logistical details of the Fix-It forum in advance of the associate conference.** These details should include format (one day, two day, etc.), budget, dates, location, food, and agenda.

6. **Select the team of associates (program managers) representing a cross-section of roles, responsibilities, and geography within the organization to participate in the forum.** The team size should be approximately ten to twenty associates, depending on the size of your company/team. I recommend that the program managers have at least two years of service with the organization to participate. Program managers will be expected to do the following:

   - Gather Fix-It ideas from the associates assigned to them.
   - Represent the ideas they have gathered.
   - Objectively evaluate the ideas without prejudgment.
   - Actively participate and prioritize the top ideas.

7. **Conduct a conference call with the program managers to ensure they understand the responsibilities of their acceptance and program participation.** This call should require no more than thirty minutes—twenty minutes to review the presentation and ten minutes of Q&A.

8. **Have program managers request Fix-It ideas from the associates assigned to them.** They should provide approximately two weeks to collect and assimilate the Fix-It ideas prior to the Fix-It forum. Conference calls, department meetings, and one-on-one discussions may be utilized to introduce the details of the program and to solicit or generate inputs. Utilize prompting questions in the meetings, such as the following:

   - What causes you the most pain?
   - What can really make a difference to the customer?
   - If you had a magic wand what would you do with it?
   - If you could remove wasteful steps, what would they be?

Associates may be provided with templates to facilitate their submission of ideas to their assigned program manager. Keep it simple. Help associates in any way to get their ideas captured as easily as possible, even if the program managers fill out the data they hear from associates.

Program managers should submit all ideas they receive. This is a critical point. All opportunities are up for consideration during the forum, and the full list should be brought to the event. At this time, the ideas should simply be organized prior to arriving at the forum.

9. **During the forum, have program managers placed in several small teams.** These smaller teams break out and begin vetting the Fix-It ideas that were captured. The program managers fully explain the ideas to their team, and the team discusses the ideas so that they are fully understood. The final responsibility prior to rejoining the main meeting is to select the top several ideas to present to the leader and to all of the program managers. The following criteria are used to shorten the list:

- Ease of implementation
- Impact on the business
- Effect on employee engagement
- Resource requirements
- Customer impact

The leader reserves the right to dismiss any idea that does not fit the intent of the "quick wins" objective of a Fix-It forum.

After the Fix-It Forum: Next Steps and Follow-Up Communications

1. The leader might consider sending a thank-you note to all of the program managers.

2. The leader or the local office champion should communicate the findings and actions from the event to all associates. This communication should provide general next steps and time-lines, without disclosing the granular pieces of the prioritized list of ideas.

3. Consider providing periodic updates to your associates, to communicate progress and success, and keep the Fix-It forum in front of everyone.

Sustaining the Fix-It Culture Going Forward

In preparation for the forum, the program managers may find that many associates refrain from submitting their ideas due to lack of time to complete the business-case forms. Consider establishing a Fix-It hotline whereby associates call the phone number and the hotline administrator asks the appropriate questions needed to complete a business-case form. The captured ideas are then forwarded to the leader or champion on a regular basis for consideration.

In order to maintain additional momentum with building a ground-up culture, holding regular Fix-It forums in the future is recommended so that the master listing of ideas, and any new ideas, can be evaluated and *fixed*!

9

Belief: Changing Culture Can Change Results Quickly

HOW A NOT-SO-POPULAR VP SUCCEEDED BECAUSE EVERYONE LIKED THE CULTURE!

Jeff Watson called me—again. *Oh, crap*, I thought. *What does he want now?* As a reminder, Jeff was the leader in Roanoke who brought me there from Huntsville. He was also the vice president of the Southeast territory, the one who had promoted me to district manager of Virginia. He had seen me succeed and grow as a leader and believed in my ability to build high-performing cultures. Jeff had been promoted to president of distribution for Trane North America. After the chitchat, he got to the point. "Jason, we have a huge hole in strategy and marketing for Trane North America. I have a role approved to fill the gap and think you might be a good candidate."

Jeff Watson's call was not a surprise. I'd mentioned in my last review that I might be ready for another challenge soon. Serving as district manager was a ball, but I thought my work there was done, and it was time for me to move on.

Long story short, I ended up taking the position. This was certainly the challenge I needed, but it wasn't necessarily what I asked for. I was leading strategy for Trane North America, and I was taking over a team of vertical-marketing leaders who, although they served similar purposes, had never really been on a team together. Two other groups reported to me in this new role. They didn't fit neatly with the other two, yet they needed a home. So, now I had vertical markets, strategy for North America, and two support functions for Trane North America.

My biggest challenge was that many of the people on the vertical-marketing team didn't really like me, because they felt excluded by what I had done in Virginia. Now, the guy who didn't need them was leading them. Boy, is that a trust challenge or what?! And, as I learned in my second role with the company, trust is key to success.

Our first team meeting was intense. It lasted two days. The first day included a manager assimilation, which was led by an experienced, yet unbiased HR leader (fortunately I had a friend in Trane who was willing to play the role). It was structured as follows: I opened the meeting and told the team that they needed to be completely candid with Sam, the HR leader, and then I left. Sam told them he was going to ask a bunch of questions, make notes of their answers, and then summarize what he heard. He told them he would never place a name with a comment unless that associate wanted him to. Once they had a chance to discuss all the questions, I would be invited back in to hear the answers as well as answer any questions that came out of the discussion.

Sam asked question such as "What do you know about Jason?" "What should Jason focus on first?" "What concerns you about Jason?" Let me tell you, as I would soon learn, the group wasn't shy. The summary seemed almost overwhelming. What we expected to last ninety minutes stretched into a half-day exercise.

Here are some of the questions I was asked: "Why did you not believe in vertical markets in your past career and now believe we are important?" "How do I know you have my back when you come from the field?" "Did Jeff bring you in here just to dismantle the group?" Fortunately, my Roanoke preparation allowed me to stay calm and be myself. I answered all questions honestly even when I didn't have an answer; I was comfortable saying "I really don't know" when appropriate. I was revisiting my initial beliefs of integrity and trust under much more intense circumstances.

Although my team-meeting schedule was blown, the time could not have been spent any better. The tension in the room was released and the productivity we gained over the next day and a half was amazing. In four hours, we had blown up the past and were starting fresh together. They had built some trust in me and I in them.

In the second half of day two, I displayed the vision and mission we were going to follow. It seemed clear to me that the vision and mission of the Trane sales offices should be common to us since we were serving the sales offices, but I stopped short of telling them the guiding principles (behaviors). Since I had just become their leader, I was unsure which behaviors would indicate this team was living the company's values. The guiding principles needed to be meaningful for this group, so I decided to open up the subject for a team discussion rather than direct what may be wrong or unaligned. To this day, I still talk about what happened next.

The team jumped into a spontaneous dialogue. They discussed the feeling of finally being a team and the power it could have for them and our company. Sarah, the HR leader, said, "We used to be on our own little dinghies, out in the middle of the ocean. Now, at least we are on one big dinghy together." "One big dinghy" became our guiding principle for putting the team first. Tres, the retail-market leader, said, "It seems our meetings and conference calls used to be all about innocuous stuff. Now, we are cutting the *muda* and getting down to details." I am still not sure what muda means. (I think it means "crap.") "Cut the muda" became our guiding principle for talking direct with respect. Toward the end of the dialogue, Laura, the health-care leader, said, "We haven't been a group known for adding a lot of value. From this day forward we should get shit done." "GSD" (externally described as "Get stuff done") was our guiding principle for focusing on results.

As I walked out of the meeting, I thought, *Associates own this culture, and this culture is going to be strong.* They had culture clarity. We had our vision, mission, and guiding principles in place and, more important, the team members completely owned achieving them because they had created them. It was time to build an enlightened team, which is exactly what we did three months later in our second meeting. We ran a revised version of the personal-development class in which all team members rated themselves and each other. Then, during the second day, we discussed how we rated our teammates and ourselves. Once again, the power of this candid discussion brought us self-awareness and respect for each other. All team members were now confident they had value to add to the team and just as confident that they needed their teammates to make the biggest impact.

Then this group of talented individuals became a high-performance team. The list of tools they created was truly extraordinary. All leaders created strategies, goals, and scorecards for each of their markets. For the first time in my memory, the marketing team had goals that were directly connected to business results, and they were holding themselves accountable to delivering on those goals. They also revised and deployed the Fix-It event we had created in Virginia across all of North America. As in Virginia, the event was culture changing, but this time it had created excellence from the bottom up throughout our company.

Once the offices started deploying the Fix-It event, we heard incredible accolades, such as "best event I have ever attended" from a thirty-five-year tenured associate. The excitement was rooted in the fact that our offices were getting things done and the company was supporting those efforts. Associates were discovering how things could be done better on their own, and those things that were beyond their control were raised up to our team, which was then changing the systems (getting shit done). An associate in North Carolina made things better for associates in California. It was truly cool stuff and a great lesson for us all. Excellence really was driven from the ground up and in a big way.

As with the other steps in my career, this one gave me a new gift, a belief that changing culture could change results very quickly. I saw it in Richmond, yet the experience with this particular team was energizing. People wanted to be great, and when given the chance, they would give their all to get there as quickly as possible. As I also learned in Richmond, associates are many times just asking their leader, "What is taking you so long?" They know that every associate can be great, their team can be great, and they can do great things for their customers and business.

CULTURE IS REAL, AND IT CAN CHANGE RESULTS VERY QUICKLY

Culture is a team's beliefs about how things get done. It guides the team members' actions and decisions. The question is, are we conscious of it and leading it, or do we let it simply exist on its own? When leaders define culture for associates, the associates become more culturally aware. As when individuals become aware of their strengths and their peers' strengths and immediately realize how to use those strengths to help the team, so it is with culture. Once a general awareness of culture takes place within a team, there is an immediate understanding of where that culture is and where it can go.

If a leader can provide the road map and guidance for a cultural-development process, the associates, with their new awareness, will take the appropriate actions. When they take actions in unison, their culture will evolve quickly.

As discussed in chapter 6, these beliefs build upon themselves to form a system of beliefs. (See figure 9.1.) The system is segmented into foundational, structural, and ultimate beliefs, which all lead to a systemic idea. You'll soon learn how the beliefs fit together to form the total business-leadership system. For now, let's look at how we have used the tools in this book to create two *structural* beliefs, beliefs that combine to form an *ultimate* belief: you must change the culture to change the results quickly.

So, how do leaders actually provide the road map? Since culture is about beliefs leading to actions, in order to change culture, we first need to change beliefs. To get there, let's first understand how people build their beliefs. Here is a picture of the ladder of inference. (See figure 9.2.) It outlines how beliefs are built. Humans take an experience and affix meaning to it. From that experience, we make assumptions as to why that experience happened and then test to see if our assumptions are correct. We then make conclusions that eventually turn into beliefs, and it is the beliefs that guide our actions.

The ladder of inference suggests three core concepts around beliefs:

1. Our current beliefs have been built from previous experiences.

2. Once a belief is in place, it guides our actions.

3. Changing our beliefs requires changing our experiences.

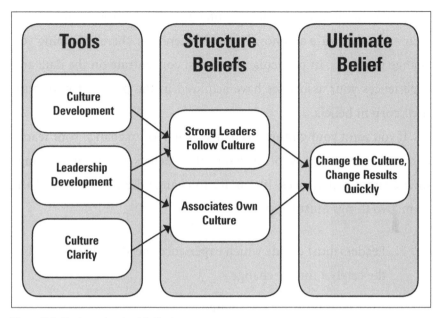

Figure 9.1: Business Leadership System

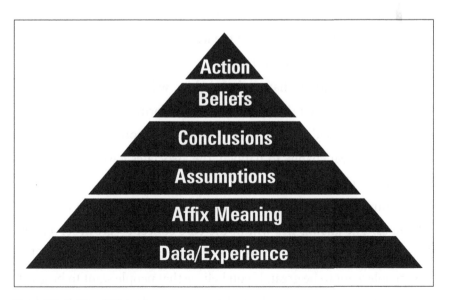

Figure 9.2: Ladder of Inference

Understanding the ladder of inference can help you understand your current culture and how it got to where it is, thereby helping you change it quickly. In particular, you must concentrate on the data and experiences your associates have acquired in the past that have built their current beliefs.

If you want your culture to change, you need to change your team's current beliefs. If you want to change their beliefs, you need to change their current experiences. If you are to change the experiences of the team, two things must happen:

1. Leaders must decide which experiences need to change and be the catalyst for the change.

2. Associates must see the change.

Both of these points are crucial and neither is easy. How things get done is highly influenced by the managers in an organization. Leaders have their own habits, which create experiences for their associates. To change the culture, you will need the leaders to do some hard work on themselves by changing some habits.

Even if the leaders change their habits, will the associates see the change? As mentioned earlier, once humans form beliefs, they tend to find supporting evidence for their beliefs and discount evidence to the contrary. For real change to happen, the associates have to be open to the reality of change.

Fortunately, there is a proven and quick path to solving these two dilemmas. The answer lies within the core concept—grow, serve, perform (GSP)—discussed in chapter 5. A foundational concept of GSP is that people want to be great. If you believe that people want to be great, then it is a natural step to believe that teams want to be great too. Once you recognize the truth in this statement, you need to bring awareness to what needs to be great within your culture to gain full commitment to making it great.

Think of it this way. A team has a natural desire to be great. If a leader points out where the team could be better—for instance, in teamwork—the team sees it for what it is and has a natural desire to get there. They are now open to a new reality. Once leaders provide the consistency of message, support, and training behind the message, the associates will see new experiences around teamwork. They will start to make assumptions that teamwork really is important. They will test those assumptions until the assumptions become new beliefs. This can all happen within six months or less.

Remember we need to provide culture clarity. We do that by defining the culture we want to have. We provide a clear vision of where we are going together. We provide a clear mission of what we do together. And we provide the guiding principles of how we agree to behave together. Once we provide that culture clarity, we pinpoint the specific changes we need to make today to ensure we are progressing toward the culture we want tomorrow. Just like my team did in the North American strategy leader role. They picked the three things that needed to be great about us going forward: team first (one big dinghy), results based (get shit done), and direct with respect (cut the muda).

When what we want to change is clear and focused, it is much easier to change. When an entire team has the same clear focus on change, the change is easy to implement. People—even leaders—hold each other accountable to changing their habits and beliefs. When it is simple to change, change happens very quickly. As do the results from that change!

IBM FROM 1993 TO 1994

Lou Gerstner was hired by IBM in March 1993 to turn around Big Blue, which was hemorrhaging cash. Many wondered why in the world IBM would hire someone without any technical background. How could someone who led a $3 billion stable company that made crackers (Nabisco) turn around a $30 billion company as complex as IBM? The challenge was larger than many people recognize. In 1992, IBM lost $3 billion. In 1993, IBM lost $8 billion. Yes, in two years IBM lost $11 *billion* dollars! (For those of you who have seen *Austin Powers*, picture Dr. Evil with his pinkie finger next to his lips.)

As we all know at this point, Lou did turn around IBM. What we may *not* know as clearly, however, is how Lou turned the company around and how quickly he did it. In 1994, IBM made $3 billion. Yes, an $11 billion turnaround in just one year. And it did not stop there. IBM continued their turnaround with an average of more than 30 percent growth in bottom-line profits for the next three years. Now that is some spectacular business results—and they happened so darn quickly.

In his own words, here's how Lou did it: "Until I came to IBM, I probably would have told you that culture was just one among several important elements in any organization's makeup and success—along with vision, strategy, marketing, financials, and the like. I came to see, in my time at IBM, that culture isn't just one aspect of the game; it is the game. In the end, an organization is nothing more than the collective capacity of its people to create value."[3]

When Gerstner started, he estimated that it would take five years to turn around IBM's culture, yet he went to work to change it right away.

3. Gerstner Jr., Louis. *Who Says Elephants Can't Dance?* New York: Collins, 2002.

His number-one focus was teamwork. He wanted teamwork to be the core of their culture. He immediately aligned compensation, recognition, and business goals around teamwork. Then he got personal. He asked every employee to have three "personal business commitments" aligned with IBM's broader goals. Performance against those goals was directly tied to salary.

The change in experience for the IBM associates was so stark that they could not help but see it. With Lou telling them that teamwork was now most important, combined with the drastic changes in compensation and recognition, the associates immediately built the assumption that teamwork was important. When they began testing this assumption, it did not take them long to confirm it.

People not willing to change left the company. All others quickly aligned their behaviors. And there is no doubt why. The culture naturally wanted to be great, and when a strong leader showed them what they could do differently to be great, they made it happen. They held each other accountable for getting there quickly. They even held managers who were not on board accountable to the new direction. Lou thought it would take five years. He way underestimated on that one.

Sure, there were tons of other things that Lou and his team worked on beyond culture. They changed their strategies and laid off hundreds of people. Over time, they shut down core businesses and started others. Yet there was one underlying theme behind all their actions. They were focused on changing the culture. In fact, Lou knew that culture "was the game." And Lou would be the first to say that he was blown away with how quickly that culture changed and how quickly the culture changed the results.

TOOLS

Culture can be developed and developed quickly with a conscious process. And, as we have discussed many times, this process can be learned and taught. It does not take a culture guru, just a leader who believes that culture drives profit and that the culture should be owned by the associates within that culture.

Culture-Development Process Overview

Now that we have all of these parts and pieces coming together into a system, we need to start looking at them as a continuum. Figure 9.3 illustrates the step-by-step process a leadership team should use to develop a high-performing culture. The first step is the most crucial. You need the leaders in the organization to have a deep understanding of culture in general and of the specific culture you are trying to create for your company. This is called "culture clarity" and was discussed in chapter 3. If your leaders are clear, then they can commit to the importance of culture and teach the rest of the associates about culture.

Once you have culture clarity, which can sometimes take multiple meetings and discussions, you need to move to culture development. In the appendix, I provide an overview of a culture-development plan with examples for Trane North America. With the plan in place, you need to make it easy to execute. As we have seen throughout the book, there are many ways to make it easy to communicate and sustain the culture-development process. From Fix-It events and culture cards to culture training for new associates, the leadership team should create the core tools that enable the leaders throughout the company to develop culture in a consistent way.

Now that you have the plan and tools in place, it is time to execute. You must place a high importance on the actions detailed in the culture-development plan. They should hold equal importance with monthly financial performance, so they should be included in monthly business reviews and leadership meetings.

Finally, you need to evaluate how you did. You might consider using a culture-measurement tool like the Denison Culture Survey to see trends in the culture. Did we impact culture as we thought? If so, let's celebrate. If not, what is the lesson learned? With a strong annual culture evaluation, you can evolve the culture-development plan for the coming year for even better results. And, as you change the culture, you will change the results quickly.

Map to Culture Development

Refer to figure 9.3 as you read the following text.

1. **What is culture?** We need training, dialogues, and a team understanding of culture. This is the first and most crucial part. Without understanding, we cannot lead. The goal is culture clarity.

2. **How do we lead?** Now that the leadership understands what culture is, they need to agree to a consistent and focused approach to leading the culture together. The goal is a culture-development plan.

   Tool: Culture-development process details and examples

3. **What are the tools?** We need to provide support material and examples that will help leaders lead the culture. The goal is ease of execution.

   Tool: Culture card example

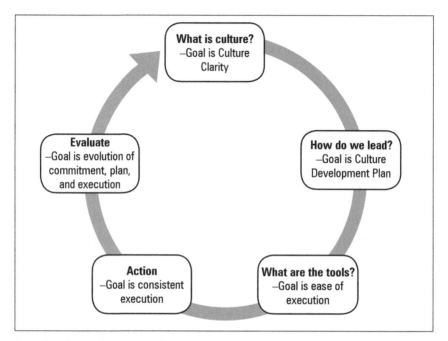

Figure 9.3: Culture-Development Process

4. **What actions must be performed?** Leaders must hold them-selves and each other accountable for action. The goal is consis-tent execution.

5. **How should we evaluate?** The leadership team should evaluate how they did qualitatively and quantitatively. The evaluation should culminate with lessons learned and a clear picture of the next phase of the culture-development process. The goal is evolution of commitment, plan, and execution. The circle then begins again.

10

Belief: Strong Leaders Follow Culture

THE CULTURE CALLED FOR LEADERS, BUT NOT ALL OF THEM ANSWERED

After nine months as the strategy leader for Trane North America, I was getting into my stride. The teamwork had increased dramatically, as did its impact on our business. It was starting to get fun.

Then, during a casual conversation while we were talking about his kids, Jeff said, "Jason, you ever thought of being a territory vice president?" *Huh?* The poor transition and surprise question caught me off guard. I was really happy as the vice president of strategy, and I thought our team was making tremendous progress. We were getting real results, yet we were not finished. *Why in the heck would he ask me that?* I thought to myself.

The current Central territory vice president was being promoted, and they were considering who would be a good replacement. Yes, Jeff Watson was again the key decision maker. Now that I think about it, I guess I would still be four roles back in Huntsville, Alabama, selling equipment and controls, if it weren't for Jeff Watson. Guess I owe that guy a lot. Jeff believed in me and thought I would be a great candidate. I, on the other hand, had my doubts.

It was not that I had doubts about doing the role. A territory vice president is the leader of district managers (two roles back for me, when I was in Virginia). I knew I could do well at the role and would learn a lot at the same time. My doubt was about which role was more important to the company. A territory VP was a prestigious role with responsibility for a $1 billion profit-and-loss statement. That even sounded cool. The strategy role I was in, although relatively new, was very important to the future of our company; I helped put strategy to the forefront of a very tactical business. And we were not finished with the important work we were doing. This new team was gathering momentum for the first time, and I owed them something more.

As in the past when I had to decide about the Roanoke general sales manager position, I wrote, thought, and prayed about what I should do. Shelby and I talked about it many times, and once again she supported me. And, like those decisions, the answer was inevitably in my heart rather than my head. I had decided after getting the district manager job that God was in control, and He had done a pretty darn good job for me up until now. The problem was discerning His direction for this decision. It was a real quandary for me, and up until the last minute, I thought I was going to decline.

"Yes, I will apply," I told Jeff. Although I was still slightly uncertain, I decided to go for the job for one reason: to see if I could build a high-performance culture for a company rather than just a district. As a district manager, I had learned a lot about building culture and even had some great success. But the district manager role happens on the ground, with the associates. I had a lot of control over the actual environment the associates worked in. By taking the role of vice president, I would be building district managers who had control over the environment. Could I take what I had learned to that level?

After the interview process, I was selected, and then I had to meet with the president of Trane North America, David Regnery, for the final vote. During the interview, David asked me, "What will be your greatest challenge in this role?" After a slight pause, I said, "Meeting your performance expectations monthly while building a high-performance culture for the long term." The official announcement was made in March.

I had created a plan for the first 120 days on the job around the beliefs I had built over the past twenty years, and I was initiating it as fast as I could. For instance, I now knew that "A" (associates) comes before "C" (customers) and "B" (business), so I made sure that my first meetings had nothing to do with business and everything to do with building trusting relationships. Now that I knew that strong leaders follow culture, I wanted every meeting in the districts to bring more clarity about culture and how each leader needed to follow it. One of the most important things I did before starting was to create a common message. From the first minute I met someone in a territory, I wanted to send a consistent message about what we would be doing together with our culture, why culture was most important, and what I needed them to do to lead it.

Every office visit in the first 120 days not only included one-on-one time with the district manager and his direct reports, it also included time with their district associates. I wanted to make sure the first step with all of these people was toward a high-performing culture. The message included a definition of culture and my commitment to keep culture a top priority. It also included a description of the "three lenses": associates, customers, and business. Yes, the ACBs were a common acronym across all Central territory offices by the end of the first 120 days.

The beliefs I had learned gave me the confidence and clarity to start by defining where we were going. And my confidence surprised even me. A little more than ten years ago, I had been walking into one of the best cultures in Trane and doing my best to screw it up. I had walked into Roanoke with a director mentality, and I had walked into my next role knowing that leaders lead rather than direct. Now I was walking into a team of high-performance leaders with a clear confidence of what we could do together. I knew the ACBs worked and that the other beliefs made it all happen.

The first Central territory team meeting was thirty days after I was officially announced. In that meeting we discussed the roles each of us played and how we would work together. We also discussed our territory's vision, which was to be the best: the best place to work, best place to buy, and best place to invest. You guessed it. It was the ACBs in vision style. Fortunately, it was also a prior vision for Trane from five years ago. Everyone on the team connected with the vision and agreed it was ours. We also spent time on leadership development in the meeting, which was the first time they experienced a high-level meeting that was focused on developing our people. It sent the message that I would personally focus on the "As."

THE CULTURE HAS THE AUTHORITY

Then we got deep into the business results. From days 75–120, we held a "deep dive" in every district. Deep dives are two-day events during which all team members are present and we dig into the details of the entire business for each district. The sessions were intense for everyone involved.

My first deep dive was in Chicago. It had some good and bad results. I'll start with the bad. For some reason, I moved into director mode and was very direct without respect. When the pressure turned up to a level I had not experienced before, I fell back on some old habits by directing more than I was leading. As for the good, the office needed a strong commitment to excellence from the ground up and our meeting certainly sent that message. They heard my passion around excellence and my belief that they needed to own it. Afterward I asked around for feedback. They appreciated my directness and commitment to excellence, yet were obviously concerned about my approach. I apologized and promised to get better at asking tough questions without attacking.

Looking back on the Chicago deep-dive experience, something occurs to me. Every leader is human. We all screw up. It is these screwups that can actually improve the culture if they are handled correctly. If a leader asks for feedback, hears it, and then makes changes from it, the entire culture sees how people learn and grow. If a leader apologizes and then learns from the experience, that same leader can expect all associates to do the same. By never putting themselves ahead of culture, leaders keep the responsibility where it should be—with the associates to own culture.

Think of it this way: the leader is always responsible for the culture, yet the culture has authority over the leader. If you have a high-performing culture, the leader should kowtow to the culture. If the culture is still being built, the leader should still act with an eye toward the future, an eye toward the associates owning the culture. Leaders must have a combination of humility and confidence. They must have confidence in the priority of culture and how to make it happen. At the same time, they must have humility in the fact that the culture they are leading takes authority over them.

Fortunately, the district manager in Chicago was gracious. I learned a lot from the Chicago experience, and by the time I got to St. Paul (my third deep dive), I was darn good at being direct with respect in a high-pressure environment. At the end of the deep dives, I was a better leader, and we were all very clear about the business strengths and weaknesses of each district. All districts created their business-improvement plans, which also included solving issues around their structures, leaders, and people. The deep dives had created ACB development plans for each office.

CULTURE TELLS YOU WHEN TO DISMISS A LEADER

One of my leaders had poor culture scores that were advertised across the company. Besides the bad publicity for him, I was worried about what it meant for his team. I dug into the Denison Culture Survey and company-engagement surveys with him. We decided we had to do something to improve the culture. To his credit, he had been placed in a situation that required tough decisions. Also to his credit, he was a very good leader who went through a very challenging economy. Yet, at the same time, the team was in a bad spot. Could he turn it around?

My HR leader, Mellisa Scaccia, was a true partner through the office visits, deep dives, and evaluations. She suggested we take a pulse survey to see if the direction of the culture had improved from the most recent culture scores. Great idea! I thought, and we immediately deployed the pulse survey. I set up a meeting with the district manager a month in advance to review the results I knew we would have by then. Four days before the meeting, Mellisa and I got the results. They were not good. In fact, they were worse than the previous scores.

As I was driving from the airport to the hotel the night before, my mind was in turmoil. The district manager was a good guy who had a poor culture on his hands. There were plenty of reasons why he was responsible, yet just as many to give him another chance. It began pouring rain, so much so that I could barely see out the rental car window. As I got closer to the hotel, it stopped, and as I approached the hotel, I saw a rainbow. Believe it or not, the rainbow ended at the hotel. Maybe it was God telling me that the right answer would become evident.

The next morning I walked into the district office with an open mind. I sat down with the district manager, and after some small talk, we dug into the details of the pulse survey. We saw the painful results together and discussed them. Being the great person he was, he was very open and candid with me about the results. We agreed the culture was in a deep hole and although he was not entirely to blame, it was there under his watch. I told him that I thought he definitely had the talent to lead a district, yet my concern was if anyone had the ability to change the tide of a culture in this situation.

"I am very concerned that it takes too long for the existing leader to turn around a situation like this. I care about you, yet there is a team of people counting on me to make the right decision here. Although this pains me to say, we need to think about what the right decision is. Allow me some time to think about it and I will get back to you soon." He was obviously disturbed, yet we both agreed this was a tough situation.

How can a leader know when it is time to replace associates or a leader? It's not an easy question to answer. When considering whether to let associates go, I first ask if they are great or improving toward greatness? If they are, then keep going. If not, keep working on helping them to become great. If they don't progress, then it is probably time to find a better spot for them.

When trying to decide whether to let a leader go, the issue is much different. Leaders are responsible for the growth, service, and performance of an entire team. They are also responsible for the culture of that team. If that leader has been in place for a while and the culture doesn't believe in him, there is usually not enough time to help that leader. You have to let the culture process make the call.

This leader was in just that spot. It was my job to follow the culture process, even though I believed this leader could be great someday. I called a few people I trusted to discuss the problem, and then on Friday told him my decision. I was replacing him.

There have been very few district managers replaced, so when it happens it rockets through the organization. Removing this district manager caused the same rumors and disruption, especially since this leader was well liked by his peers. We replaced the district manager with a very talented young leader with huge potential. Within six months I had visited the office three times and the feedback was amazing. The people were very excited about the new direction, and the marked improvement in energy level was palpable. Nine months after the change, we did another pulse survey, and the culture had gone through the roof. By the way, the business results of this office also changed very quickly. The leverage (bringing revenue growth to the bottom-line profit) this district achieved the following year was in the top 10 percent of the offices in North America.

THE ACBs ARE A SYSTEM OF BELIEFS

With more influence and authority in Trane North America, I began weaseling my way into culture discussions with other leaders and HR. One of these discussions was about Trane's guiding principles. Guiding principles are the behaviors that indicate we are living the company's values. Going back to our definition of culture—a team's beliefs that guide its behaviors and actions—the guiding principles are the defined behaviors we expect in our culture. In other words, the guiding principles play the crucial role of specifically telling the organization what behaviors we expect. They are spoken in words that relate to how associates behave every day in their real jobs. This provides culture clarity. It also provides culture development because not all of a team's beliefs will align with the guiding principles we expect to see.

In Trane's case, we were owned by Ingersoll Rand (IR), which had defined a set of values for the entire enterprise: integrity, respect, innovation, teamwork, and courage. It was time for Trane to determine the guiding principles that were aligned with those IR values. Knowing that guiding principles were a cornerstone of strong cultures, I volunteered to lead the leadership committee that would decide on the guiding principles across all of Trane North America.

This team began holding conference calls immediately to define our goal and a plan to make it happen. The plan was pretty simple. We would ask our people across North America what behaviors they thought Trane had or should have that would indicate we were living each of the five IR values. We would then combine and reduce our list to a maximum of fifteen guiding principles (three for each value). Each leader on the team surveyed his or her segment of the organization, and then we worked to combine and reduce. Within a short period of time, we had a great list of guiding principles.

Back at the Central territory, things were going well. By that time, I had visited all the offices twice. We also had our second team meeting, which started with a discussion about culture. I went through the vision again, and this time added a mission and the newly defined guiding principles. I showed the connection between the three: the vision being *where* we are going together, the mission being *what* we do together, and the guiding principles being *how* we agree to behave. That defined the where, what, and how of our culture. We discussed the idea that these three elements made up culture, and if we were consistent as a team, we could use them to develop an even stronger culture. We decided we should make a culture card so that all associates could keep our vision, mission, and values in the front of their minds.

We also discussed excellence being driven from the ground up and what that meant. Specifically, with planning and budget season right around the corner, we decided that we were going to do things differently that year. Instead of the budget and plans being given to the offices, the offices were going to build them from the ground up. By building them from the ground up, the plans would be better and the teams much more committed. During our second meeting, I outlined the new process for building budgets and plans from the ground up. The team was cautiously optimistic about this new approach.

The results from the budget-process change were powerful. As I mentioned, normally the budget goals are given to the office by corporate, which means they usually don't make much sense when they get to ground level. The offices then scramble to figure out how they can get even close to the bottom-line target, which makes the budget somewhat meaningless throughout the year. This year was different. For the first time in my career at Trane, every office had an achievable budget that was directionally correct for how they should run their business. We were actually using our budget to evaluate how any office was doing in its improvement plans. This result was a true indicator to me that excellence is driven from the ground up.

On day two of our meeting, we spent the first two hours in "the speed of trust" leadership development. This was a class I had adapted from Stephen Covey's *The Speed of Trust: The One Thing that Changes Everything* for training on my first two beliefs—integrity and trust. The book did a great job of defining trust, and I brought it to a business perspective. The training included real-life Trane examples, dialogue questions composed for this audience to consider, and exercises that were meaningful for my team. The feedback from the class was very positive. As the meeting ended, there was some real excitement in the air. We were clearer about culture and what we needed to do as a team to develop the culture we desired. There was also clarity about excellence being driven from the ground up.

After the meeting, I stopped and assessed the company progress to date from my standpoint as vice president of the Central territory. We had reviewed all but grow/serve/perform and enlightened teams. All the leaders had bought into the priority of culture and were quickly advancing how to lead it in their offices. But there was still something I needed to figure out. These beliefs, which I had learned one by one over eleven years, did not stand on their own. They worked together. They were a *system of beliefs*, and if we were going to be successful, I had to figure out how to lead them as a system rather than individual beliefs. How could I expect these leaders to lead the system of beliefs in their offices when I was just figuring out how they all fit together? If I could put it all together, this team would go farther than I might have imagined.

The fallout from my decision to remove one district leader was waning and the team was starting to gel. We had created our culture cards and distributed them to every office. I had also done a town hall meeting in every office that communicated the vision (ACBs), mission, and guiding principles to all associates in our territory. Our culture development was well under way, and the commitment from the district leaders and staff was palpable.

Toward the end of the year, we deployed the Denison Culture Survey to every district in the Central territory. We then reviewed the results and created plans for each district and at the territory level. Monthly, as we reviewed business results, we also reviewed our progress on these culture plans. The leaders were leading the ACBs, and it showed in their monthly reviews.

As it turned out, the watershed moment for the district managers and me occurred during this time. As I mentioned, the team was both excited about our direction and stressed about the departure of one of its peers. Concern was growing about me "not being in the same boat" with the district managers. I started to hear rumblings from the district managers, and it was time to address it head on. We were coming together for the third North America district manager meeting soon, so we tacked on a meeting of the Central territory district managers with me before the national meeting. I asked one of the district managers, Randy, to gather and consolidate feedback and facilitate the meeting.

When the day came, I got up at 3:30 a.m. to catch a 5:20 a.m. flight. I then attended my boss's staff meeting from noon until 6:00 p.m. Our Central territory meeting was scheduled for 7:00 p.m. at a private room in a restaurant. As I was walking from the hotel to the restaurant, I realized how tired I was. I stopped and said a little prayer: "Lord, please give me the energy, patience, and listening power, so I can be who I need to be in this meeting."

We got to our private room, ordered drinks, and opened up with small talk. After ordering our meals, it was time to dig in. Randy opened with a statement devised to butter me up: "Thanks for setting up this meeting and for your willingness to hear our feedback. We want you to know that we are excited to have you as our leader and see this as another positive step." With that out of the way, he jumped into the feedback, and there was tons of it. It was about me, about Ingersoll Rand, and about Trane executive leadership. It was direct, and it was with respect. Some of their concerns were legitimate and others were things that had happened in the past, yet were now resolved. I listened, asked questions, and commented when it was appropriate.

We cleared away most of the concerns about IR and Trane and got more specific about me. We danced around the issue until Randy added his summary comment: "Jason, we don't think you are in the boat with us. It feels like you are outside the boat judging rather than in the boat leading." I thanked Randy for his courage and asked if he or anyone else at the table could provide some examples of how I sent that message. They brought up email messages that were mainly one-liners that indicated a director mentality. They also brought up the deep dives and fear about how I had decided to remove their peer.

Again, I thanked them for their candor. They could see that I was tired, yet engaged. I said, "Allow me to tell you what is in my head when I send email to this team. I think of you as talented leaders. When I send email, I don't think you need much detail, and I am more interested in your thoughts. I don't mean to direct. In fact, I mean to hear what you think. It is my fault I have sent the wrong message with my email, and I am sorry. I will do better at adding words around what is in my head and my intent going forward." The tension in the room seemed to blow out the door. It was a relieving moment, yet we were not done.

"My decision about your peer was not easy. Can you tell me more about your concerns in how I made the decision?" I asked. Mark, the district manager for Ohio, spoke up. "Why did you not try to mentor him to success?" I put my head down, looked back up and said, "That is a great question and one that I considered for a long time. At the end, I decided that he had dug a deep hole with his culture. It would take a while to change the beliefs and behaviors he used to dig the hole, and it would take even longer for the culture to trust him again. It would not be fair to him, yet most important, I didn't think it would be fair to the team of people he was leading."

With that brief discussion (it lasted until 11:30 p.m.), we had cleared away many of the concerns of the team. We all realized we were in the same boat, rowing in the same direction. I ended the meeting with the following comment: "I believe in each of you. I commit to helping you be even better leaders in the future." Smiles abounded as we left the room. As I look back, that meeting was the pressure-relief valve for our team to get to the next level of enlightened teamwork. More importantly, I realized that checking to see if the leaders themselves follow the culture—even when that leader is you—is one of the final linchpins of putting all the culture beliefs into a system.

The power of what was happening in the Central territory needed to happen throughout Trane. I reached out to my territory vice president peers, both of whom had been previous bosses of mine, one of whom was Felix. I suggested that we needed to hold hands on the vision, mission, and guiding principles. They were both natural culture leaders. They agreed and thought the idea of culture cards was great. They ordered culture cards for every office.

Next it was time to get consensus with the North America team. I modified my culture presentation and asked if I could deliver it at the next North America district manager meeting. David Regnery agreed, and Lisa Knapp, the North America HR leader, and I ended up speaking to all district managers in North America for two hours about culture. At the same time, many from David's leadership team were present and got their first introduction to this approach. The awareness throughout our company was growing quickly, as was the excitement about focusing on culture for our business.

After speaking about culture to many different teams in many different venues, I generally receive a common response. No matter the history of the team or the roles they play in the organization, people naturally connect with culture discussions and beliefs. There is no debate about its importance. Teams want to be great, and when they have clarity on how to be great, they go there naturally. I think it's interesting that it seems so risky for a leader to lead with culture rather than business. The reality is that the associates can't wait for leaders to lead with culture.

The Central territory ended the year with substantial business results. We surpassed financial expectations for the first time in many years. We achieved the highest rates of return and the highest growth in productivity. We were making more money as a percentage of revenue than any other territory, which had not been the case the year before. Most importantly, we were moving the culture quickly—which was moving our results quickly. The plans we had created were getting done, and you could feel the difference in the territory team.

CULTURESHIP: PUTTING IT ALL TOGETHER

With the success of the previous year behind us, we were much more confident heading into the coming year. It was time to dig deeper into our grow/serve/perform belief and our enlightened-teams belief. With my experience in the VP of strategy role, I was ready to deploy the feedback process we created in that first personal-development class back in Roanoke.

The first Central territory meeting of the year was a doozy, and it was all about our people. We planned to start our year as we start our culture—with the associates and leaders. The meeting had four sections. The first section was about culture. I demonstrated the latest culture presentation so that they could deliver it to their teams. It included the vision, mission, and values and the three specific values we were going to focus on this year. This would provide the focus that would move our culture up a level.

What happened next really surprised me. I had planned for the culture discussion to last ninety minutes. It ended up lasting almost three hours and was driven by the questions and dialogue from the team. Culture was hitting home with every member of the team, and they were ready to get much deeper into how to build high-performance cultures and how to be great culture leaders. These leaders were following culture.

The second section of the team meeting focused on the leaders within the districts, those who reported to the district managers. We created a tool that we used to evaluate the leaders within the districts. We then discussed all these leaders as a team and decided which were high-potential leaders and which needed help.

The third section of the team meeting worked on building stronger leaders in my Central territory team—district managers and staff. To do this, we had a full day of coaching training so that each of us could be a better development coach to our people and our teams. We also trained in how to lead rather than direct.

The fourth section of the team meeting introduced grow/serve/perform (GSP) through experience. I knew that if we added GSP to our culture-development process, we would create an enlightened team. We each had filled out a rating sheet on ten leadership characteristics for each of the individuals on the team, including a self-rating. Then, like we did in the Roanoke personal-development class so long ago, we talked straight with each other. On day three of our team meeting, every member of the team gave their self-ratings and then listened as their teammates gave them their ratings. As I had seen many times before, the self-awareness was powerful, as was the awareness of their peer's talents.

As had happened in the past, when the exercise was done, the energy in the room was markedly higher. All participants felt good about themselves. Yes, they had weaknesses, but so did everyone. Everyone in the room had heard from everyone else in the room about his or her strengths. Each felt important. It was equally significant that people recognized each other for their strengths. When the feedback was done, one of the leaders, Randy Krampe, asked an important question: "Jason, how do we take this knowledge of talent awareness to the next level for our team? Can we do something more substantial to ensure that we are using all of the talent in this room to its utmost?"

We answered Randy's question together and came up with a pretty cool process for leveraging our team's strengths. Without going into the details, the team would work together to develop and achieve the annual focus areas. For me, his question was a pinnacle moment. He was essentially saying, "I am great, I believe my teammates are great, and I want to use our skills to create the high-performing culture we all know is possible." He was saying that he wanted us to grow, serve, and perform as a team. And the answer from the team was, "We want to too!" They were becoming an enlightened team.

We were starting to put the beliefs together into a system. It happened almost naturally. As we learned the power of each belief and started practicing them in real time, we saw the need for the other beliefs. The one driving belief was the ACBs. If we believe that purposeful associates inevitably drive our business, then we must continually ask ourselves how to help our people be great. We would certainly have to act with integrity, give them trust, lead rather than direct, and ask them to make everything we do better. We would also expect them to grow, serve, and perform.

To create a team of purposeful associates, the ACBs drive us to expect associates to own the culture and to develop that culture to a high-performance level. To do that, we need teams of associates who are clear on the culture we are trying to develop and even clearer on their role in making that happen. In other words, we need enlightened teams. When we truly buy in to the ACBs, we put together the system of beliefs that make it happen.

CULTURESHIP LEADS TRANE GLOBALLY

On Friday, February 24, my boss, David Regnery, held a North America leadership team meeting. In between the North America district manager meeting and this meeting, I was given the opportunity to speak about culture a few times to this team. At the end of the previous year, we had decided that "Create a Winning Culture" would be one of our three key strategies for the next three years. It was now time to have the team discuss how we would achieve this strategy together. The North America leadership team was ripe for culture clarity and culture development.

David asked me to present for an hour on culture to start the meeting. I was on slide two when the first question came up. There were four more questions before I could get to slide three. As with my latest Central territory team meeting, this team wanted more information about how they could lead culture. The hour turned into two hours. David's leadership team was ready to follow culture.

I will forever remember that day for one main reason. Every leader in Trane North America, from engineering to manufacturing to accounting to human resources to every territory in distribution, asked to have culture cards. We had one culture card for our entire company, and we all agreed to create a high-performance culture together. We had changed Trane across the nation.

Since then it has started going global! I am now on the global culture committee and have most recently delivered the culture-building process to leaders across the globe. It is unclear where these lessons will take our global leaders, but beliefs this strong will change the world sooner or later.

As I look back on my incredible experiences in my latest role, I see strong confirmation of the system beliefs I have been taught over my career. It is like, "Holy cow this stuff really works!" I also see the gift of one additional belief: strong leaders follow culture. As a leader of a company, one of the most crucial decisions is about which leaders are on your team. Leaders are the leverage point for culture. They must have the crazy combination of confidence and humility. They must be strong enough to lead the culture and strong enough to let the culture have authority. The right leader will have the culture running itself quickly. The wrong leader will never get there.

STRONG LEADERS FOLLOW CULTURE

For me, leadership boils down to two questions: "Is the individual a strong leader?" and "Do they follow culture?" I have found that strong leaders *do* follow culture. Of course, if a culture is in a bad place, then the leader has to step up and lead the culture to another place. But strong leaders should still follow the image of what the culture could and should be rather than letting the culture become about them.

There is a huge difference between a leader who is strong enough to follow and a leader who requires the team to follow him. The difference is humility. Humility means knowing you are human and prone to mistakes and misunderstandings. You can have confidence in your capabilities to lead, but you must always be humble enough to follow when it's appropriate. However, humility by itself will not drive you to excellence. Strong leaders are clear on where the culture could and should be and have a personal confidence that the team can achieve that state of excellence. They are confident to lead the culture while always giving authority to the culture.

What is a strong leader? In their book *The Extraordinary Leader: Turning Good Managers into Great Leaders*, John H. Zenger and Joseph R. Folkman describe the difference between a good leader and a great leader as having one strong competency versus having four strong competencies. In fact, their studies conclude that not having any weaknesses puts leaders in the thirty-fourth percentile of leadership effectiveness. Having just one strength moves them to the sixty-fourth percentile. That's right, one good strength puts you in the top 40 percent of leaders! Having three strengths moves leaders to the 81st percentile. Since four strengths is the eighty-ninth percentile and five is the ninety-first percentile, you can easily see that four strengths is just about all a leader needs to be one of the best in the world.

Think about that. First of all, it says that the goal is not to be strong in every competency. Instead, the goal is to recognize where we are strong and make that area even better. The second message is that becoming a strong leader is not some magic formula only available to the privileged few. It is just four competencies! If we can have the discipline to develop the strengths we have and add one or two more, we can be a great leader. It's not simple, but it's well within reach.

Zenger and Folkman then prove this thought by showing statistics around business results between good and great leaders. Leaders who are in the eightieth to eighty-ninth percentile have the following results compared to those in the thirty-ninth percentile or lower:

1. 15–20 percent more employee engagement

2. 50–100 percent more net profit

3. 50–100 percent less turnover

4. 50–400 percent more commitment from employees (intention to stay)

5. 50–400 percent more customer satisfaction

These are dramatic results for going from good to great in leadership and substantial proof that leadership leverage is real. This is really the substantiation of our belief that leaders don't direct, they lead. Yet strong leadership is only one answer. We could have a strong leader in place whose team performs well while she is in the position, yet as soon as we replace her, the business performance lags. True leadership is leaving a legacy of performance well beyond that leader's departure. In other words, if leaders were truly focused on doing the best thing for the organization, they would desire the performance of their team to continue well beyond their departure. They would want a culture that was based in high performance to sustain that performance. This requires us to ask question two: does the leader follow culture?

Leaders who follow culture have humility. They know that excellence is driven from the ground up. They know that associates own the culture. They know that the end goal is enlightened teams who are driving the change in culture, which will drive and sustain premier business results. When you have leaders who lead and follow culture, you have the right leaders in place.

This is why our newest belief, strong leaders follow culture, becomes so important. The culture takes the precedence. "Strong leaders follow culture" is a summation of two lessons I learned in my career—that leaders lead and leaders follow culture. Appropriately, my career path taught me first that leaders lead. Then, as I started to learn the importance of culture and how to lead it, I learned that strong leaders follow culture.

TOOLS

Leadership development is a core pillar for creating a high-performance culture. The biggest influencer on culture is the leader. Knowing this, each team or company must put a focus on developing its leaders. Again, the good news is that professionals are not needed for the most part.

Leadership Development

What follows is an outline for a leadership-development class that should be deployed at least annually. Even if all the leaders have gone through the training, a refresher short course can be reviewed annually as a part of the leadership team meetings throughout the year. The goal is to have every leader proficient with core management tactics that enable an ACB culture to exist.

The training should be insourced, meaning that someone internally should facilitate it to ensure that it is connected to the specific business and that it lives beyond the course. If you facilitate within the company, you tend to create something that is "yours" and has a life of its own rather than something owned by some "outsider."

To make it easy to facilitate the training internally, make the format of the class different than the traditional training process. The traditional process has experts come in to provide "teaching." This course uses internal facilitators to host dialogue learning. The difference between teaching and dialogue learning is powerful and, as it turns out, dialogue learning is a more effective way to learn.

Dialogue learning is rather simple to facilitate. Essentially there is a short PowerPoint created on a core leadership topic. The facilitator runs through the first five to ten slides that explain the topic. Since the slides are rather self-explanatory, the facilitator does not need expertise. The next few slides are in the form of questions. Each of these questions is about the leadership topic but does not have a right or wrong answer.

For instance, you might be talking about feedback but ask the class, "Why do leaders tend to tell rather than ask?"

Obviously there is not one correct answer to this question, and that is where the dialogue comes in. By asking the question, you will start to pull thoughts from the class. As those thoughts bounce around the room, a better understanding of the topic at hand happens naturally and more thoroughly. People become actively engaged in the learning process, which makes the learning much stronger. It also makes the learning more applicable.

My experience indicates that one person within a company who is passionate about leadership yet not necessarily a leadership expert can start the leadership training through this concept of dialogue learning. Through the dialogue, this one person can train the facilitator of the next dialogue. Eventually, leadership development becomes a system of discussions that happen naturally and consistently.

Next is an outline of a leadership development class using dialogue learning:

Step 1: Pick your team. First you must pick your students of leadership. These people must be those who are either in leadership positions or are the up-and-coming leaders. There should be no more than twelve people in the group, including the leader/facilitator.

Step 2: Set your price of admission. All students must commit to the course. They must also do some homework. Reading books or attending courses is generally the two preferred admission tickets. Good book choices include

- *First, Break All The Rules: What the World's Greatest Managers Do Differently* by Marcus Buckingham and Curt Coffman
- *Developing the Leader Within You* by John Maxwell

- *Top Grading: How Leading Companies Win by Hiring, Coaching, and Keeping the Best People* by Bradford Smart
- *The Extraordinary Leader: Turning Good Managers into Great Leaders* by John H. Zenger and Joseph R. Folkman
- *Execution: The Discipline of Getting Things Done* by Larry Bossidy, Ram Charan, and Charles Burck
- *The Fifth Discipline: The Art & Practice of the Learning Organization* by Peter Senge
- This book!

Divide up the assignments so a diverse set of perspectives is achieved.

Step 3: Hold your first meeting. The guidelines and road map should be decided upon and shared. Give a copy of this plan to each participant. Discuss leadership versus management. The group members should also choose their standards of excellence. The standards should include, among other things, attendance, cell phone usage, and active involvement. At the same time, your group members should choose meeting dates and times. I suggest that your team meet at least twice monthly. Finally, each participant should provide book summaries on the books they read to all other participants before the meeting begins. Homework is for every member to list the five most important skills of a leader-manager.

Step 4: Open up the dialogue. The first class is an open dialogue about what it takes to be a great leader-manager. Every team member should communicate their top-five list, allowing for discussion and even a summary of the team's top ten. The goal is not to create a list so much as it is to have a discussion of what it takes to be a great leader-manager.

Step 5: Practice team building. Homework for this class is to read *Five Dysfunctions of a Team* by Patrick Lencioni. This class will be devoted to team building and the dynamics of creating a cohesive high-performance team. The team members will discuss each chapter of the book and then decide what they will do to build their teamwork.

Step 6: Getting the right people on the bus. The next few classes will go through the tactics for getting the right people on the bus, taking the wrong people off the bus, and putting all the people in the right seats. Topics will include interviewing, hiring, first ninety days, GSP, handling people issues, and redeploying. Homework is to rate all direct reports as A, B, or C players on the talents of integrity, trust, and excellence.

Step 7: Work on talent development. The people-building class deals with using the talent-development tool to assess and build talent. Direct with respect, the three questions, and 360 feedback will all be discussed. Homework is to identify three strengths of each direct report or team member.

Step 8: Make a plan. The next step is individual planning. Demonstrate the company personal-development and performance-management planning processes. This class will also deal with the plans themselves, including characteristics of good and bad plans, the execution of plans, and following up. Distribute example plans. Homework is to develop an individual planning form for one direct report.

Step 9: Set expectations, measurements, and accountability. Clarity of expectations is critical. Clearly defining the role, associated responsibilities, performance, behaviors, and planning execution should all be discussed. Also discuss the leader's responsibility to work with team members to develop the right measurements for his or her role, including what to measure, how to measure it, and different examples.

Finally, accountability, a key word for all leaders, should be discussed. Homework is to use existing role descriptions to develop clear expectations for each role in the leader-managers' departments with associated measurements.

Step 10: Prepare reviews. This step covers how to structure a review, how often, how to give feedback, 360 reviews, how to discuss the past, how to discuss the future, revising plans, and following up.

The process ends with a graduation and a big personal thank-you from senior management.

11

Results Are the Real Starting Point

SLOW SALES HAD EVERYONE POINTING FINGERS, BUT A CULTURE SNAPSHOT REVEALED THE REAL CULPRIT!

Results are not the end. They are the beginning. Contrary to many management gurus, financial results alone do not tell you what is right and wrong in the business. Results are indicators of something that is right or wrong with your *Cultureship*. And a careful look at your ACBs will reveal the real story. Business results help guide our progress on culture by identifying where the ACBs are working and where they need some improvement or support. This might seem like a minor issue of semantics at first glance, but it can be a profound change in thinking and leading for managers, as it was for me.

A great example is the Central territory results six months after I took over. During the first quarter of the year, we had some real sales issues in our service and contracting businesses. Rather than making rash decisions, we decided to use these results as indicators of something that was wrong within the system of beliefs. The fact is that whatever is wrong can be tied directly to a breakdown with one or many of the beliefs in the system.

As an entire team, we dug into the service and contracting business with an eye toward our associates and our customers. We found structural problems in some areas, leaders who were directing rather than leading in other areas, and a lack of training or support for our associates in many areas. With these core issues identified, we put plans in place to get them corrected. By the time the third quarter rolled around, we had the business issues resolved, and our efforts were starting to show up in our numbers. The growth of our service business and our contracting business had risen dramatically. My boss was impressed.

This was a revelation for the entire Central territory team. In the past, we may have put too much emphasis on the business side of the ACBs to solve financial problems. This time we took a balanced approach and found beliefs within the system that needed attention. When we fixed those beliefs and behaviors, our results changed. We had learned that business results were indicators of something right or wrong with our Cultureship.

POOR SERVICE-BUSINESS RESULTS LEAD TO ACB OPPORTUNITIES

A district office within Trane was having issues with its service business. Although the business was growing overall, the number of non service-agreement customers and the amount of purchases for the past three years were both down. Although the decrease in profit was a cause for concern, the customer segment often became service-agreement customers, who generally made much larger purchases, so their future business was at stake too.

The district manager, who believed that excellence was driven from the ground up, called together a team of associates to discuss the issue. He prepared them all with the data and opened the meeting by describing the issue and why it was important. Then he suggested that there were three buckets that could be affecting this issue, and he wanted everyone's thoughts on each of the ACBs. The service manager thought that maybe it was the A bucket because the technicians were too busy to "drop by" these customers anymore. The team dug into the data, and it did turn out that technician productivity had gone up, but not by much. The service-sales leader thought it also might be the A bucket because the compensation plan might not incentivize this leg of the business. Again, further questioning and dialogue revealed that this was unlikely, and the salesperson in the room agreed that was not an issue.

Finally, the service administrator suggested that they dig into the customer bucket. She asked how the customer figured out whom to call when they had an HVAC problem. The salesperson realized it was a good question and asked who within the customer's company actually made the call to their service company to fix their HVAC unit. The team decided that many times it was the receptionist or administrative people within the customer's business who were asked to call someone to fix the HVAC. After a while, they realized that in the past, these customers probably used the Yellow Pages and today probably used Google. The service manager pulled out his computer and Googled "HVAC Service" for their town. The results were revealing: Trane was not listed in the first three pages.

The team decided to get marketing on the case to see how they could get Trane on page one and listed as number one if possible. They also asked the service administrator to start asking new customers why they called Trane to get a better understanding of the influencers. Finally, after marketing was successful in getting Trane on page one of searches, they agreed to measure the number of new customers calling per month to see if there was a change in behavior as a result of their actions.

Three months later they were very certain they had solved the problem because the number of new customers increased dramatically. The following year, they grew this segment of their business for the first time in three years by over 20 percent.

This is a small example of unexpected results being indicators that there is something to learn within the ACBs. The leader in this example pulled a team together, provided clarity of the unexpected results, explained why it was important, and made sure the three buckets were explored. The team dug deeper into each thought by asking more questions and using open dialogue to find the right answer.

Someone using results as decisions rather than questions might have reduced headcount in this area or decided to replace salespeople or even shut down this portion of the business. The financial problem would have gone away, yet no real solution would have been discovered.

FINANCIAL RESULTS SHOULD PROMPT QUESTIONS

It is finally time to talk specifically about business results. Although we have discussed business results in the previous chapters, it has been in relation to other factors. It was from the "if you do this, then you get business results" perspective. We have spent ten chapters on how to achieve business results. Now it is time to discuss what you do with the results you achieve.

It is easy to get caught in the "leaders can manage results" loop. Besides the fact that we all came to leadership as individual contributors, leaders prove their ability to add value by moving the business needle when needed. The leader is constantly pressured to meet monthly and quarterly projections. As the end of the quarter gets closer, a leader might hear from her boss, "I need you to drive additional operating income to help out your peers." How is a high-performing leader supposed to say no to this request from his boss?

So the leader does what she can. She cuts cost and drives revenue. Both of these options, when solely focused on the short term, can hurt the long term and have a negative impact on culture through the lost time spent on reactive actions versus added-value service. The pressure to be a valuable leader to the company is actually pressure to be a poor leader for long-term results.

There is a dirty little secret we need to discuss: leaders can't manage results. Leaders can only directly manage results in the short term, and doing so is many times counterproductive. Assuming that leaders are not selling to customers, there are two main tools a leader can use to manage short-term results: cost reduction and price reduction. Managers can reduce people and cut other expenses to reduce the costs within their business and increase short-term results. Leaders can also decrease the price in the market to increase demand. Considering that price reductions degrade margin, the overall "management" of operating income from price reductions is minimal. Therefore, the main tool a leader can use to manage short-term results is cutting cost. Although cutting cost is appropriate in certain circumstances, it has a high likelihood of hurting long-term results when only focused on the short term.

Yet from a long-term perspective, there are no options for managing business results directly. The only answer to managing long-term business results is to follow the ACBs. Leaders are constantly managing business results by managing structure, employee productivity, and costs, but there is a difference between good management *delivering* good results and directly *managing* results. In fact, this may be one of the most prevalent mistaken beliefs that exist in business leadership today—the belief that I as a leader can manage long-term results directly.

In Marshall Goldsmith's *What Got You Here Won't Get You There*, Peter Drucker, author of more than thirty books on leadership and one of the wisest leadership experts of our time, said it this way: "We spend a lot of time teaching leaders what to do. We don't spend enough time teaching leaders what to stop. Half the leaders I have met don't need to learn what to do. They need to learn what to stop." Leaders need to stop thinking like an individual contributor who directly affects results and more like a leader who gets things done through others.

Marshall Goldsmith, a well-known and highly acclaimed leadership author and consultant, also lists the twenty habits leaders must stop as they transition from individual contributors to leaders. The number-one habit to stop is winning too much. Marshall says that the drive to win and achieve at all costs, which probably helped us succeed as an individual contributor, is a killer for leadership. Leaders must step out of the direct connection to results and allow their associates to succeed and fail, so that the organization can grow.

I personally believe that when Jim Collins, in his famous book *Good to Great*, described level-five leadership as "a paradoxical blend of personal humility and professional will," one of the points he was making is that level-five leaders never took credit for success and they didn't jump in front of their people to directly impact results. In his words, "Their ambition is first and foremost for the institution, not themselves." Great leaders work their tails off to make the organization great, knowing the results will come.

From an ACB perspective, we recognize that business results are the direct impact of customer loyalty, which directly translates from associate engagement. If this is the case, then how can we look at results as anything other than indicators? Results are the indicators of our associate engagement, customer loyalty, and business alignment.

A THEATRE USES RESULTS TO REINVENT ITSELF

Mill Mountain Theatre was facing unparalleled challenges. Building up a debt of $750,000 over the last ten years was causing an enormous weight on the financials. Now, the economy was diving, which reduced attendance to unsustainable levels. With its current earned revenue versus contributions at a 60/40 ratio (the goal is 40/60), the theatre was in a death spiral.

The new executive board met constantly to try to resolve the situation. It didn't take too long before the suggestion to close the theatre was thrown onto the table. With Mill Mountain being a shining star of their community for over forty years, this was obviously a very emotional issue. It was also well known that there were no known examples of a theatre closing and reopening. Was the board deciding the death of the community's beloved theatre forever?

The work the board did to understand the ACBs within the theatre helped clarify the decision. They interviewed associates, customers, contributors, community constituents, and many others. They also looked at the business model of other theatres to understand if success was possible and what success might look like. The associate, customer, and business feedback and insight helped the board build a strategic plan, including financial statements that represented that strategic plan.

The board went back to this plan to help answer the paramount question of closing. From this work it was clear that the theatre needed to close. Yet it was also clear that closing was the first step to making the theatre alive and sustainable in the future.

The strategic plan built through the ACBs directed the tough decision, yet it also provided clarity on what would happen next. And, for the first time to my knowledge, a theatre that closed came back to life. Two years later, Mill Mountain theatre opened its first full season since the shut down. This is the power of a strong ACB approach to results.

THE SYSTEM OF BELIEFS

Once you have learned all of the beliefs, you'll find that they come together in a specific way to form Cultureship. All the beliefs you have learned are a part of a greater system. You can rearrange the beliefs to form more of a working view of the total picture of Cultureship, the ACBs of business leadership. These beliefs have three levels.

There are the **foundational beliefs**—(a) integrity leads to profit (chapter 1), (b) trusting others expands profit (chapter 2), (c) excellence is driven from the ground up (chapter 8), and (d) leaders don't direct, they lead (chapter 4). These four beliefs must be foundational within the culture and leadership before any of the other beliefs can take root.

Next there are the **structural beliefs**—(a) everyone wants to grow, serve, and perform (chapter 5), (b) associates own the culture (chapter 3), and (c) strong leaders follow culture (chapter 10). The structural beliefs take the foundation to a whole new level of individual and team awareness, performance, and leadership.

As the structural beliefs take hold, we move to the **ultimate beliefs**—(a) enlightened teams achieve superhuman success (chapter 6), (b) changing culture can change results quickly (chapter 9), and (c) purposeful associates create loyal customers who maximize business results (chapter 7). When the ultimate beliefs exist, so does business success. These are the beliefs that transform an organization.

The final belief is the **feedback belief**—results are the real starting point (chapter 11). By looking at results as feedback, we create a culture of continuous improvement. Even if there are changes in leadership—or other changes, for that matter—the culture will survive and thrive.

The foundational beliefs are like creating a level and plush football field. They are the ground on which every player plays the game. The structural beliefs are like the football plays that the team calls, either on defense or on offense. They are the coordination between the players. The ultimate beliefs are the winning attitude and perfect execution a team has in the game. When you have ultimate beliefs, your football team will win most of the games, and you will achieve huge business success. Finally, the feedback belief is reviewing the film to coach the players and make changes to the plays. It is the homework that makes you better in every game. Eventually the belief system creates a dynasty football team. Your team wins year after year because they have a culture of continuous improvement.

We can also sort the system of beliefs according to their relationship to each other. By combining our foundational beliefs around integrity (always doing the right thing for others) and trust (empowering others), we form the foundation of our Everyone Wants to Grow, Serve, and Perform structural belief. By combining the trust belief with excellence (always striving for the best from the ground up), we form the foundation of the Associates Own the Culture belief. And when we combine our excellence belief with the Leaders Lead belief (leadership is to coach and lead the way rather than direct the way), we get the foundation of our Strong Leaders Follow Culture structural belief.

Now, you can see the structural beliefs are based around the three entities of associates, leaders, and culture. The structural beliefs also form the structure of our ultimate beliefs. For instance, when we combine the individual structural belief of Everyone Wants to Grow, Serve, and Perform (individual purpose) with the cultural/team structural belief of Associates Own the Culture (team commitment to success), we build the structure of the ultimate belief that Enlightened Teams Achieve Superhuman Success. And when we combine the structural beliefs of Associates Own the Culture and Strong Leaders Follow Culture (showing the culture where and how to be great), we get the ultimate belief of Changing Culture Can Change Results Quickly.

Finally, when we have enlightened teams within strong cultures, we build the ultimate belief of Purposeful Associates Create Loyal Customers Who Maximize Business Results. The total system is presented in figure 11.1.

As you can see, for each level in the system, we have tools that help leaders develop and grow that belief within their culture. Consider these tools the "coach" of the football team.

THE BEGINNING OF YOUR CULTURESHIP

I truly believe there is no end to where the ACBs could take you and your business. The Central territory blew away the first quarter budget for the first time in four years. More importantly, our company has

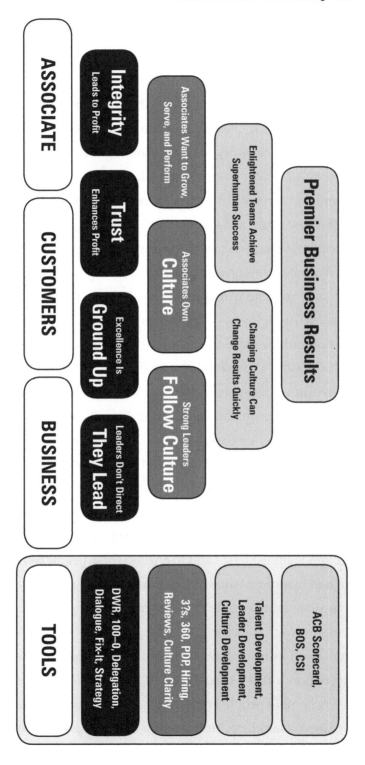

Figure 11.1: Purposeful Associates Create Loyal Customers Who Maximize Business Results

committed to the ACBs through our common vision to be the best place to work, the best place to buy, and the best place to invest. I know that a commitment to the ACBs will lead to the system of beliefs, and that a system of beliefs can lead to amazing things—for our entire company.

In the Central territory, we are becoming mature culture leaders very quickly. All district managers are taking culture development into their own hands, making it their own responsibility. Some have even created their own signs and awards about our vision, mission, and guiding principles. We have started the personal-development class in three districts. We have also started and completed a leadership-development class for our frontline managers. The consistent feedback from that class was, "What took you so long? This was great, and I want more." Most importantly, we have built the system of ten beliefs in each of the district leaders and Central territory staff.

Just recently, Shelby and I ran the half marathon course in the "toughest marathon in the nation," the Blue Ridge Marathon. It is actually in Roanoke, Virginia, and there are some *very* steep and long climbs. We trained for three months and on the day of the race, we felt ready and excited to take it on. At 7:00 a.m., we were standing together at the starting line when the announcer said, "Let's start cheering for the runners that left at 2:30 a.m. to complete the first of two marathons."

"Are you kidding me?!" I said to Shelby. These people were running the toughest marathon twice! We were only running half of it once. To me it was yet another sign that no matter how much you learn, there is always more growth possible.

I know my future holds more growth and possibly more beliefs. My latest revelation is that I need to be an "inquisitive leader" to find out the lessons in other people's experiences. I'm not sure if there is a new belief in there somewhere, but I am sure that I am still learning. I have also taken home the lesson about leadership being about my entire life, not just my professional life. My wife is now my best friend—and I am not just saying that. There is no one I would rather spend time with than her. And the same can be said of my kids. I love them as my children, and I love them as my companions. I have even started teaching the ACBs of culture leadership at my church with rave reviews.

My anticipation to see where this takes us has me jumping out of bed after over twenty years at Trane. Something great is going to happen, and I can't wait to see it. I know it is going to happen because I believe.

TOOLS

Knowing that these systematic beliefs will maximize business results, strong business leaders can use leading indicators to create a Cultureship scorecard.

Cultureship Scorecard

Now that you have seen how the beliefs come together to make a system, let's discuss how we can use this system to measure success and create the feedback loop for your business. In other words, Cultureship leaders make sure that the metrics they are using to define business success are well beyond the financial metrics alone. They know that associate satisfaction is a leading indicator of customer loyalty, which is a leading indicator of the financial results. Knowing these leading indicators exist and directly translate to business results, leaders can create a customized Cultureship scorecard for their business that applies a balanced pressure to the metrics around associates, customers, and business rather than just business results.

Figure 11.2 is an example of an ACB scorecard. In the left column is the ultimate belief that is being built through the foundational and structural beliefs. In the second column is the foundational and structural beliefs we are trying to measure. In the next three columns, we list a metric for associates, customers, and business that would indicate our

Ultimate Belief	Foundation and Structure Belief	Associate Metric	Customer Metric	Business Metric
Enlightened Teams	Integrity Drives Profit	% Personal Development Plans	Customer Satisfaction Index	Revenue growth verse market growth
Enlightened Teams and Change Culture: Change Results, Quickly	Giving Trust Enhances Profit	Revenue/Headcount	%GM—Trend	Operating Income/Headcount
Change Culture: Change Results, Quickly	Excellence is Ground Up	Number of Ideas Submitted in Fix-It Forums	Cost of Quality	Operating Income/ Headcount as percent – trend
Enlightened Teams	Associates Want to Grow, Serve and Perform	First-Year Attrition Rate	Market Share trend	% of Associates Considered High Performers
Enlightened Teams and Change Culture: Change Results, Quickly	Associates Own Culture	High Performer Attrition Rate	Number of 5+ Year Customers Lost	Team Performance Verse Peers
Change Culture: Change Results, Quickly	Strong Leaders Follow Culture	Voluntary Attrition Rate	Customer Satisfaction Index by Leader	% Leaders > Budget

Figure 11.2 ACB Scorecard

performance for the associated beliefs. You can use this example to create a customized Cultureship scorecard that stresses the foundational and structural beliefs for your organization.

Many of these metrics are self-explanatory, but I would still like to explain some of them:

- Personal-development plans (PDPs) should be created for every associate in your company. This metric measures the percentage of your associates that have a personal-development plan.
- Customer satisfaction index (CSI) can be measured and should be one of your ACB scorecard metrics.
- First-year attrition rate measures the attrition rate of associates that have been with your company for less than one year.
- High performers should be identified throughout your company. No matter how your company identifies top performers, you should measure the percentage of them versus the total population as well as the attrition rate of this very important group.
- Voluntary attrition rate is the percentage of associates that left the company through their own decision versus a manager removing them from the company.

Although you may want to pick different metrics for your business, the outline and example metrics should help you get started on your own ACB scorecard.

Now the actual results come in. During business reviews, the financials and ACB scorecard should be discussed to find metrics that are beyond expectations (either higher or lower). The results that are different from those expected should be discussed and acted upon in an enthusiastic manner. In fact, there are seven core behaviors leaders and leadership teams exhibit when dealing with the results of their business:

1. **Look in the mirror first:**

   - Create self-development plans, because the results are a reflection of your leadership and the culture you are building. When unexpected results arrive, leaders ask, "What am I doing that caused this?" and "What am I not doing that could have prevented this?" (assuming a negative result).

   - Direct discussion with leaders reporting to you about their leadership and culture. For leaders of leaders, the results must spur a candid discussion about the indication these results have of each leader's style and the culture they are building. The leaders must vocally and visually take ownership of finding the lessons and modifying behavior to change future results.

2. **Map who owns which results.** Have you been clear on who owns what? Which people or teams are responsible for which results? Is there clarity in the organization of this ownership? Are they structured, staffed, and supported to achieve these results?

3. **See unexpected results as lessons for the team.** Where there is a difference between expectations and actual results (good and bad), there are lessons. Leaders see the process of finding root cause as a learning opportunity for the organization and therefore want as much of the organization involved as possible.

4. **Dive deep into the results that exceeded or fell short of expectations.** These deep dives are always done as a dialogue between all who touch the results. When faced with a result that is out-

side expectations, leaders ask a lot of questions. They are almost always excited to learn something new.

5. **Decide what action needs to happen and/or what behaviors need to change.** Deep-dive discussions cannot end until next steps are defined and owners of those next steps assigned. The end goal is clarifying which behaviors or processes need to change.

6. **Define leading indicators to these results.** By defining leading indicators, you can see if the behavior changes and processes you chose in step 5 are actually happening. You can also confirm that these behavior changes will change the end results.

7. **Define where strategies should be changing results and define the leading indicators to those results.** You must stay proactive as well. If a leader is going to hold her team to their strategies, she must know if they are progressing in the right direction.

Leaders and leadership teams then combine steps 6 and 7 into modifications or additions to their ACB scorecard, thus ensuring that the lessons learned become cultural to the organization.

Cultureship Plan

Cultureship is the highest form of leadership. It is leadership with the purpose of building a high-performance culture that thrives and survives well behind the tenure of the leader. The end goal of Cultureship is creating a team of purposeful associates that creates loyal customers who maximize business results. In this book, you have learned the eleven beliefs that are required to achieve Cultureship personally and as a company. You have also learned tools that can help each of you become Cultureship leaders.

The beliefs fall into four levels:

1. **Foundational beliefs**

   - Integrity Leads to Profit
     Tools: Direct with respect (DWR) training, 100%–0% training
   - Trusting Others Expands Profit
     Tools: Delegation training, dialogue training
   - Leaders Don't Direct, They Lead
     Tools: Three-questions training, 360-feedback train-

ing, personal-development plan (PDP) training

- Excellence Is Driven from the Ground Up
  Tool: Fix-It event

2. **Structural beliefs**

   - Associates Own the Culture
   - Everyone Wants to Grow, Serve, and Perform
     Tools: Talent-review process, hiring process
   - Strong Leaders Follow Culture
     Tool: Leadership-development training

3. **Ultimate beliefs**

   - Enlightened Teams Achieve Superhuman Success
     Tool: Personal-development training
   - Changing Culture Can Change Results Quickly
     Tool: Culture-development process
   - Purposeful Associates Create Loyal Customers Who
     Maximize Business Results
     Tool: Business operating system (BOS)

4. **Feedback belief**

   - Results Are the Real Starting Point
     Tool: ACB scorecard

Focusing on the tools themselves, here is a handy breakdown based on the time it takes to implement and integrate these tools into your Cultureship. They can be organized into four categories:

1. **Tactical training:** Tactical training is more about awareness of tactical leadership than true behavior changes. It is usually delivered in one class. This training can be delivered in monthly

leadership discussions, on conference calls across the team/ company, or during the team meetings.

- Direct with respect
- 100%–0%
- Delegation
- Dialogue
- Three questions
- 360 feedback
- Personal-development plans

2. **Strategic training:** Strategic training goes beyond single or tactical behaviors or issues. It is much broader and deeper in scope and, therefore, takes much more than one class or session. This training should be provided at least annually to all associates and leaders.

- Personal development
- Leadership development

3. **Tactical processes:** These are processes within the company that are easy to deploy and require little modification once deployed.

- Hiring
- Talent review
- Business operating system (BOS)
- Fix-It event

4. **Strategic processes:** These processes are strategically critical to the company and evolve at least annually, requiring an annual review of the process.

- Culture-development process
- ACB scorecard

So, how do you get all of this done? This is the essentially the same question as "How do you eat an elephant?" And you know the answer to that one: "One bite at a time." Yet this is much smaller than an elephant. Here is a suggested timeline and steps to build Cultureship within your team or organization:

Months 0–3

Define the current state of culture and leadership. Walk around often. Have lunches with associates and leaders. Hold meetings where the only discussion question is "How are we doing?" Make notes for the entire ninety days about the current state of leadership and culture.

Months 4–6

1. Hold a leadership and/or culture team meeting. Pull the leadership team together to start the culture-building process. The goal is to complete step one of the culture-building process within three months.

2. Review your hiring process with HR and ensure it matches the hiring process discussed in this book (chapter 5). Put in place "stop points" to make sure the process is being followed.

3. Create your talent review process and review with the leadership team. Ask them to review all of their people with the talent review tool.

Months 7–9

1. Complete steps 2 and 3 of the culture-building process with your leadership and/or culture team.

2. Assign a leader who has a natural affinity for leadership and is in need of a "project" to pull together the tactical training mentioned earlier with the goal of delivering one of these classes per month starting in three months. Obviously, this book provides the basis of the training.

3. Assign two leaders to pull together the personal-development class to be delivered in four months. The leaders should have different personalities with at least one of them being very organized. Again, this book provides the basis for the training in chapter 6.

4. Assign HR leader or similar partner to create leadership-development class (chapter 10).

5. Create your ACB scorecard and review with the leadership team for their feedback (chapter 11).

Months 10–12

1. Complete the final section of the culture-building process by scheduling the first culture review, instituting the new-associate culture review, and having your first culture survey or measurement.

2. Prepare for your first Fix-It event as described in the book (chapter 8).

3. Start the monthly leadership dialogue with the tactical trainings.

4. Start the first personal-development class.

5. Start the first leadership-development class.

6. Feel the momentum and celebrate!

7. Notice the change in business results already happening and celebrate!

Months 13–15

1. Review/modify the ACB scorecard.

2. Define the business operating system as described in this book (chapter 7 and next in the appendix).

3. Hold your first Fix-It event.

4. Hold your second culture review.

5. Look at results as the real starting point of the next phase for your culture.

BUSINESS OPERATING SYSTEM

In the ACB approach, under each of the three buckets of associates, customers, and business, there are tools and processes (some of which were described previously). Each of those tools and processes has specific action items that must be completed to make them happen. The goal of the business operating system (BOS) is to make it easy to stay ahead of these action items and create excellence in executing them. To do this, the BOS breaks down those key actions by month.

The BOS is usually an excel spreadsheet with four tabs: associate, customer, business, and action summary. Figure A.1, the first worksheet, lists the BOS for the associates.

Moving from left to right, the high-level processes are listed in the far left column with more details about them and the goal of achieving them listed next. Then, the actions to get them accomplished are shown in the next column. The last column lists the month when the action should occur.

As shown in figures A.2 and A.3, the worksheets under the customer and business tabs are similar.

CULTURE-DEVELOPMENT PROCESS

Building a high-performance culture is actually a process that can be learned and taught. Think of this ability as a tool to change the culture, so that you can change results quickly. This is the execution phase of that ultimate belief. Once you are committed as a leader to building culture, you need to learn this process and start the building the culture you desire. Next we have created the culture-building process, including specific examples. Use this as a guide for your own plan.

Winning Culture through Culture Clarity

Define your organization's vision, mission, and guiding principles. As discussed in chapter 3, the first step in the culture-development process is to provide culture clarity to the associates. Once they are clear on where you are going together, what you do together, and how you agree to behave together, they will own making it happen.

A. **Vision:** *Where y*our team is going. Your team's vision should be aligned with a corporate vision, and there should be clarity from that connection. Said another way, your team's vision should be the more specific language that shows how it can help achieve the corporation's vision. For example:

- Trane North America's vision is "To Be The Best—Best place to work, best place to buy, best place to invest."
- Its connection to the IR vision is that being the best is a direction rather than a destination. It speaks directly to "sustainable progress" and "enduring results" with words that resonate for Trane.

B. **Mission:** *What* your team is doing. Your team's mission must be purposeful. It should incite passion from your team. Your

Hiring	**One of the most important processes** • Properly identify required competencies • High success in selecting people with culture and competency	
	HR to review and improve hiring process	January
Talent Development	**Objective measurement of every associate** • People are what drive our business • Hold high level on performance • Hold high level on support, training, career path • Put people in the right seats	
	Modify Talent Development tool	October
	Distribute TD tool to managers	November
	Rate every associate on TD tool and submit to DM/HR	December
	Talent Development Manager's Meeting	January
PMP/PDP	**Clear plans, expectations, and measurements and accountability for every associate PMP** **PMP (Performance management plan)** • MBOs (Management by objective) aligned, focused on teaming and in PMP • Qrtly reviews except for parts and service (2–3/yr) • Most associates have incentive/bonus directly tied to PMP **PDP (Personal development plan)** • Focused on strengths and weaknesses • Use competency tools	
	Prepare for year-end review	November
	Hold year-end review—end prev yr	December
	First draft of MBOs by all managers with peer feedback	January
	Associate submits PMP plan	January
	Manager approves plan or holds another meeting	Feburary
	First quarter review/PDP discussion and plan	April
	Second quarter review (PMP and PDP)	July
	Third quarter review (PMP and PDP)	October
	Finalize PMP including rating (also PDP review)	January
Culture	**Sustaining and Enhancing our Culture** • Vision, Mission, Guiding Principles (VMGP) • Communication—weekly, Qrtly, push/pull, from Mngr. • Completion of culture plan	
	Quarterly new associate culture meeting	March
	Quarterly new associate culture meeting	June
	Quarterly new associate culture meeting	September
	Bi-Annual all associate culture meeting/Mid-year update	August
	Quarterly new associate culture meeting	December

Figure A.1: BOS for the Associates

Leadership Development	**Growing leadership throughout the territory**	
	Leader feedback Stop/Go/Continue	January
	• Grow leadership within our managers	
	Leader team assessment—5 disfunctions	January
	• Self-awareness, culture core issues, change	
	Leader team peer feedback exercise	January
	• Cultural core issues—DWR, respect	
	Select LDI (Leader development), LDII participants	May
	• Grow future leaders	
	Hold LDI, LDII introductory class	June
	Every manager creates succession plan for leaders	January
Communica-tion	**Communication of progress and corporate message**	
	EEI updates	Monthly
	• Update EEI Initiative progress	
	1st Quarter All-associate update	May
	• Financial progress	
	2nd Quarter All-associate update	August
	• Corporate update	
	3rd Quarter All-associate update	November
	• Innovations and teamwork	
	4th Quarter All-associate update	February

Figure A.1 (Continued)

Strategies	**Create and confirm 3 year strategies** • Company goal is to serve customers • Find what they need • Define our hedgehog • Put the two together to find new strategies to serve	Gather market trends — January Review VOC (voice of customer) — September Complete SWOT — March Confirm core — March Confirm vision — March Team meeting to define/confirm strategies — March
Strategic Projects	**Closing projects that are strategic to our business** • Early identification of Strategic Projects • Fostering teamwork • Identifying Strategic Accounts • Goal is 75% closure rate of Strategic Projects	VM (vertical market) targeting — January VM Association review and event planning — January Strategic project and account review — January Strategic project and account review — March Strategic project and account review — May Strategic project and account review — July Strategic project and account review — September Strategic project and account review — November
Voice of Customer	**Directly connecting to customer needs** • Knowing what is working today • Knowing what is not • Understanding our competition better • We are serving customers or those who do • Recognizing trends • Identifying future opportunities • Assure we focus externally	Manager FTF (face to face) with strategic customers — Monthly Evaluate and modify customer survey — May Distribute customer survey — July Combine customer feedback — August

Figure A.2: BOS for the Customers

Account Management	Using teamwork to provide world-class service	
	Review and modify all account tiers	February
	Review and modify all account lead assignments including team accounts	February
	Review and modify all account lead assignments including team accounts	July
	Confirm peer review completion for all selected accounts	August

Figure A.2 (Continued)

	Develop the Annual Operating Plan (AOP)		
AOP Development		Associate survey	May
		Survey results	June
		Small Team VOA	August
		Big Team VOA	September
		Complete VOB (maturity path)	September
		Planning Meeting	October
		Finalize Annual Operating Plan	November
	Create the coming year's company financial budget		
Budget		Headcount changes due	August
		High-level template distributed	July
		High-level financials discussed in meeting	August
		High-level submitted	September
		Detailed budget due	November
		Meeting to finalize detailed budget	November
		Final budget submitted	November
	Execute the AOP plan		
AOP Execution		AOP update	February
		AOP update	April
		AOP update	June
		AOP update	August
		AOP update	October
		Final AOP Update	December

Figure A.3: BOS for the Business

	Manage the business to achieve annual goals	
Manager Meetings	Business meeting/Talent Development	January
	Business meeting/Strategies	March
	Business meeting/Leadership development/OLR Succession planning	May
	Business meeting/Budget	August
	Business meeting/AOP	October
	Local managers meeting—PDP training	February
	Local managers meeting—change management training	April
	Local managers meeting—communication skills training	June
	Local managers meeting—coaching training	July
	Local managers meeting—hiring & interviewing training	September
	Local managers meeting—PMP training	December

Figure A.3 (Continued)

team's mission must also be aligned with the company or corporation's mission. Think of it as the level deeper of your company's mission. For example:

- Trane North America's mission is "Making Buildings Better for Life—The life of the building, the lives of the people, and businesses in the building."
- Its connection to IR purpose is that the mission speaks directly to the "quality of life" and "safe, comfortable, and efficient" with words that resonate for Trane.

C. **Guiding principles:** *How* your team does what it does. These are the behaviors that indicate your team is living the corporation's values. It takes the corporation's values to specific behaviors that resonant for all associates in your team. Trane North America's guiding principles, for example, are

- *Respect:* (1) Safety always; (2) Trust first, understand, then act with urgency; (3) Appreciate, celebrate, and leverage uniqueness
- *Integrity:* (1) Do the right thing (associates, customers, business); (2) Deliver the highest quality; (3) Practice full accountability
- *Teamwork:* (1) Team up, down, and across; (2) Recognize, celebrate, and have fun!; (3) Earn empowerment by knowing your business
- *Innovation:* (1) Keep a positive mental attitude; (2) Be open to new ideas; (3) Be the best by continually improving customer value
- *Courage:* (1) Communicate direct with respect; (2) Challenge the status quo and embrace change; (3) Take calculated risks

Use the following road map when creating your vision, mission, and guiding principles.

- The vision and mission can be drafted by the leader and/or leadership team. It should then be tested and evolved through feedback from all constituents within the region.

- The guiding principles should be drafted by the associates. A simple survey that defines "behaviors," provides examples, and then asks for their opinion of what behaviors indicate that you are living each corporate value. This feedback should be collected from all sub-teams. A culture subcommittee should take the feedback and reduce it to a maximum of three behaviors per value.

- Once the vision, mission, and guiding principles are in final draft form, an executive team meeting should be held to make any finalizations as a team.

Winning Culture Communication

With the vision, mission, and guiding principles set in stone, it is time to gather understanding and commitment throughout the organization. As discussed in chapter 4, leaders lead by passionately and consistently communicating culture through

A. **Culture presentations:** Create a core culture presentation (five slides max) that starts all meetings held by high-level leaders to communicate the vision, mission, and guiding principles.

B. **Culture cards:** Create culture cards for every associate in your team.

C. **Culture dialogues:** Open culture discussions with leadership teams, associates, etc.

D. **Leadership communication toolkits:** Provide all leaders with a communication toolkit that ensures consistent delivery of the culture message.

Winning Culture Development

Now it is time to move the current state culture to future state (winning

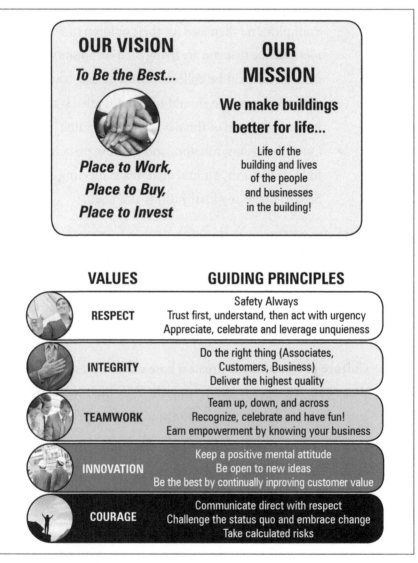

Figure A.4: Sample Culture Card

culture). As discussed in chapter 10, strong leaders follow culture by gaining clarity on what could be better in the future. The best way to do this is to define what must be different.

A. Have the leadership team evaluate the guiding principles and choose the top three that need to be improved in the coming year.

B. Edit the slide to highlight these three guiding principles.

C. Have all leaders communicate these three principles with the culture circle. (See figure A.5.)

D. Create a "culture maintenance" program that ensures continuous communication and development of the winning culture. For example, hold a monthly leadership call for all leaders/managers within your region.

Winning Culture Commitment

This is where the rubber hits the road. Is culture development a flash in the pan or a long-term commitment of your company? Strong leaders make sure that the culture-development process is a consistent and continual behavior within the organization that survives and thrives well beyond any leadership changes.

Now that you have created the definitions of your culture around vision, mission, and guiding principles (VMGP), it is time to make a concerted effort at bringing the VMGP to life within your company, thus consciously leading the culture to where you want it to be.

Culture can be changed quickly, and a change in culture can make a substantial change in your business results. It just takes leaders who are committed to the vision, mission, and guiding principles. By keeping the vision, mission, and guiding principles simple, you make it easier for leaders to lead the culture-change process.

So, if you set your vision as the "best place to work, best place to

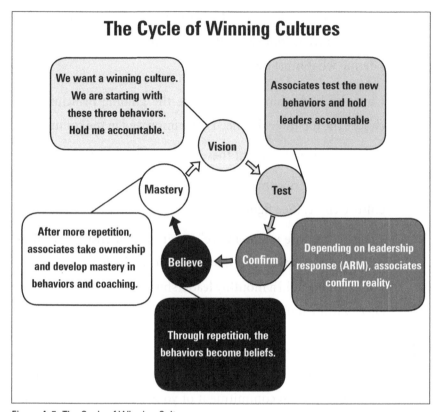

Figure A.5: The Cycle of Winning Cultures

buy, and best place to invest," you ask your leaders to constantly choose the ACBs and communicate around them. They should ask, "How does this affect our associates, customers, and business?" with every decision. This simple act starts to move the culture quickly.

If your mission is "to inspire and nurture the human spirit—one person, one cup, and one neighborhood at a time," you ask your leaders to reference this mission with every piece of feedback and coaching they provide their associates. Leaders recognize and reward by this mission as well. Again, consistency creates clarity and commitment. Clarity and commitment create results. And results can happen quickly.

If you have five to ten guiding principles and there are two you have decided to focus on in the coming year (e.g., be direct with respect and the team comes first), then you ask every leader to start meetings with examples of how associates have lived these principles. Send communication that highlights the importance of these principles. Reward people for living these principles.

Most importantly, hold leaders accountable to living the VMGPs themselves. Leaders are the greatest influencers on culture, so they will decide if the vision, mission, and guiding principles are important or not. If they decide they are and live them consistently, culture moves quickly. If not, culture moves as it wishes.

Here are three suggestions to help leaders lead the culture and to hold them accountable:

1. **Hold twice-annual culture reviews.** The leader of the organization travels to all teams/locations to hold short meetings completely focused on a culture review. The leader repeats the VMGP and provides explanation behind all. The leader also asks for feedback from associates on how they are living the VMGP.

2. **Hold new-associate culture meetings.** Every new associate sits down with the leader of the organization within the first month on the job to discuss culture. Develop a standard presentation to communicate the culture. This is when the associate gets his or her culture card.

3. **Take a culture measurement.** Measure the culture of the organization annually with a culture measurement tool and make plans for improving the culture. Use this tool to spot check culture in individual teams and to determine if feedback indicates

there are cultural issues.

These three steps taken with ownership and commitment from the leadership team will sustain the culture-changing process. Combined with the culture card, posters, and general communication, culture will drive your business results substantially.

Index

A

ACBs (associates–customers–business performance), 97–107
applying to a theatre, 177–78
caring associates, 104–5
and cultureship scorecard, 183–87
as driving belief, 161
and enlightened teams, 97–100
overview, 101–3
for revealing root of problems, 171–74
tools, 105–7
See also Cultureship Plan
ACBs, enrolling district leaders in
associate development, 145–47
as Central territory vice president, 143–45, 153, 155, 156–57, 158, 180–82
company-wide culture clarity, 145

deep dives, 147–48
dismissing a leader, 148–51
accountability. See authority; responsibility
American Society of Quality Control, 105
Anderson, Matte, 114–16
annual events, 106–7
ARC International's "100%–0%" approach to life, 11, 14–15, 56–57
associates, 29–42
attrition rate, 185
creating excellence, 113–14, 122, 133, 147, 153–54, 173
and customers, 102, 104–5
employee training sabotaged by managers, 49–50
engagement of, 77, 114
firing with GSP focus, 78–79
fitting the person to the job, 70–71, 74, 77–79, 98
"Fix It" forum, 118–19, 121–27, 133
and hiring process, 83

hiring tool, 81–83
interviewing potential new hires, 82, 83
learning something new every day, 117
natural desire to be great, 137, 139, 158
ownership of culture, 35–38, 115–16, 132, 148
perfectionist and pushover bosses, 52
strengths of, 70–71, 73–74, 88
talent review tool, 79–81
assumptions, 7–9, 12, 135, 137
attrition rate, 185
authority
of culture, 147–48, 162–65
and delegation tool, 26
establishing expectations, measurements, and accountability, 169
for results, 11–12, 23
and trust, 22–23

B

behaviors
  claiming responsibility for results, 11–12, 14–15
  human sensitivity to, 7–9, 21
  justifying or blaming others, 10–11, 14
  performance as alignment of skills and, 75
  See also skills; talents
beliefs
  building on each other, 161
  building our, 134, 135, 136–37
  and culture, 36
  feedback belief, 179, 190
  and problems with results, 172–74
  See also system of beliefs
beliefs, false, 7–8, 12
Bingham, Sara, 52
Birmingham, Alabama, 1
blaming others, 10–11, 14
Bohm, David, 27
Bolton, Dorothy Grover, 95
Bolton, Robert, 95
Bossidy, Larry, 167
BOS (business operating system) tool, 106–7, 194, 196–201
Buber, Martin, 72
Buckingham, Marcus, 75–76, 82, 93, 167
budget process, 153–54
building automation systems, 17–20
Burck, Charles, 167
business-improvement plans, 148
business operating system (BOS) tool, 106–7, 194, 196–201
business results. See profit
business review metrics, 103

C

career plans, 80, 81
CCAP (community college access program), Roanoke, Virginia, 91
Central territory, 143–47, 153, 155, 156–57, 158, 180–82
Central territory vice president, 143–47, 153, 155, 156–57, 158, 180–82
change process, 113–14
changing the current culture, 129–42
  beliefs and, 133–37
  breaking through preconceived notions, 130–31
  building an enlightened teams, 132–33
  cultureship leading the way, 158–65
  defining current culture, 40–41
  dialogue on guiding principles, 131–32
  IBM, 138–39
  introducing vision and mission, 131
  planning and budget process, 153–54
  presentation to North America team, 157–58
  tools, 140–42
Charan, Ram, 167
Chicago, Illinois, 147–48
choices, 5. See also integrity
coaching
  "do it my way" versus, 33
  helping people to be great, 66, 68–71
  leading goals, 53, 54–55
  from leverage point, 48, 51
  personal-development plans, 56, 59–62

teaching district managers, 159
Coffman, Curt, 75–76, 82, 93, 167
collaboration, 14
Collins, Jim, 37, 38, 93, 176–77
commission, about, 2
communication
  about vision, 54–55
  collaborating, 14
  common message, 145
  culture communication as part of Cultureship Plan, 203–4
  dialogue tool, 27
  follow-up to Fix It forum, 126
  listening, 14
  and personal-development plans, 59–62
  sharing your intent, 13
  speaking your mind, 13
  talking candidly about individual results, 74
  three questions tool, 55, 56–57
  See also entries starting with "Personal"
community college access program (CCAP), Roanoke, Virginia, 91
company systems tool, 42
competency
  core competencies for each role in company, 81–82, 83
  improving strengths, 163–64
  trust as combination of character and, 22
  unconscious culture competence, 65
  unconscious to conscious level, 38

See also skills; talents
conscience, 7–10
contracting business, large, 89, 98–100
contracting business, small, 86–87
controls-estimating process, 23–24
core competencies for each role in company, 81–82
core processes, 106
cost cuts, effects of, 175
Covey, Stephen, 22, 154
creative tension, 53–54
CSI (Customer Satisfaction Index), 185
cultural wizardry, learning, vii–viii
culture
    authority of, 147–48, 162–65
    awareness spreading to willing ears, 158, 159–61
    culture-building process, 120, 162, 192–93
    culture cards, 45, 153, 157, 162, 204, 207–8
    culture consciousness development, 114–16
    culture consciousness effect, 116–20
    culture-development process, 89, 119, 140–42
    culture reviews, 112
    culture team, 115–20
    Denison Culture Survey, 119, 146, 148–49, 155
    excellence as cultural, 51–55
    "Fix It" forum, for continuous improvement, 118–19, 121–27, 133
    and hiring process, 82
    influence on leaders,

37–38, 55
    leader inclusiveness, 31–32
    leaders' influence on, 36, 51, 55
    as lever versus leverage point, 45–50
    natural desire to be great, 151
    ownership by associates, 35–38, 115–16, 132, 148
    permeating the company with, 43–44
    politics of a bad culture, 38–40
    and profit, vii
    and strong leaders, 162–65
    and teamwork, 44, 45
    tools, 41–42
    unconscious competence, 65
    See also ACBs; changing the current culture; entries starting with "Personal"; strong leaders and culture
culture clarity
    company-wide, 145
    and culture-development process, 140
    Cultureship Plan, 195, 202–3
    from guiding principles, 152
    and high performance teams, 86
    Newbern's creation of, 40
    self-awareness and, 89
    for team development, 97–98, 99, 137
    cultureship, viii–ix, 158–62, 180–83. See also system of beliefs
    Cultureship Plan, 189–207
    beliefs, 189–90

business operating system, 106–7, 194, 196–201
    culture commitment, 205–8
    culture communication, 203–4
    culture development, 204–5, 206
    culture-development process, 195, 202–5
    timeline, 192–94
    tools, 190–91
    See also culture clarity
cultureship scorecard, 183–87
customers
    and business results, 177
    customer service, 97–98, 99–100, 104–5, 113–14, 117
    and high performance teams, 87
    long-term relationships versus quick profit, 6
    loyalty of, 104–5
    support of and working together, 4–5
    trust of, 2–4
    See also ACBs
Customer Satisfaction Index (CSI), 185
"cut the muda" as guiding principle, 132

D
decisions
    and ACBs, 102
    empowering others to make decisions, 23
    justifying or blaming others, 10–11
    taking responsibility for, 11–12, 14–15, 113

See also authority;
responsibility
deep dives, 147–48
DeHart, John, 50
delegation tool, 25–26
Denison Culture Survey,
119, 146, 148–49,
155
destiny, 72
Developing the Leader
Within You
(Maxwell), 167
development. See entries
starting with
"Personal"
dialogue learning, 166–69
dialogue tool, 27
directing, leading versus,
49–50, 55–59, 65–66,
71, 156
direct with respect (DWR)
tool, 12–14, 26, 94,
95, 132, 148, 167–68
do the right thing. See
integrity
draw and draw debt, 2
Drive (Pink), 23, 71
Drucker, Peter, 176
DWR (direct with respect)
tool, 12–14, 26, 94,
95, 132, 148, 167–68

E

emotional intelligence, 27,
66–67
Emotional Intelligence
(Goleman), 66
employees. See associates
employee training
sabotaged by
managers, 49–50
empowering others, 23
engagement, 77, 114
enlightened teams, 85–96
developing a student
retention
program for
high schools,
90–91
grow, serve, perform
mentality, 88–89
overview, 100

Personal Development
I and culture
clarity, 86–87
team spirit, 85
tools, 91–96
Trane North American,
132–33
Virginia district team,
89
See also teamwork
estimating process, 23–24
evaluating culture changes,
142
excellence, 109–27
associates attraction
to, 147
change process, 113–14
as cultural, 51–55
and culture
consciousness,
114–20
customers' interest
in your
commitment to,
104–5
and foundational
beliefs, 179–80
gaps in, 64–65
ground up delivery
of, 113–14,
122, 133, 147,
153–54, 173
perfection versus, 52
spreading personal-
development
process in
Virginia district,
111–12
standards of excellence,
94, 167–68
team members
choosing
standards of, 94,
167–68
tools, 122–27
Execution (Bossidy, et al),
167
external/extrinsic
motivators, 71, 72
Extraordinary Leader,
The (Zenger and
Folkman), 163–64,
167

F

facilitator of dialogue, 27
family life
half marathon course
in Blue Ridge,
182
improvements after
near breakup,
120
lice, 33–34
moves to LaCrosse and
Birmingham, 1
move to Huntsville, 17
moving to Virginia,
30–31
need for attention to,
100–101
and overtime, 17–18
Sara's vision of
timeliness, 52
Shelby threatening to
leave, 117–18
warm and loving, 183
fate, 72
fear as motivator, 71
feedback
360 feedback tool,
55–56, 57–59
from Central territory
district
managers, 156–
57, 158, 180–82
as growth mechanism,
77
and personal change,
66
in Personal
Development I,
67, 94–95
training leaders, 169
See also results as the
starting point
feedback belief, 179, 190
Fifth Discipline, The
(Senge), 53, 72, 167
financial results,
examination of,
174–77
First, Break All the Rules
(Buckingham and
Coffman), 75–76, 82,
93, 167
first year attrition rate, 185

Five Dysfunctions of a
    Team (Lencioni), 168
"Fix It" forum, 118–19,
    121–27, 133
Fix-It forum champion,
    123, 126–27
Folkman, Joseph R., 163–
    64, 167
foundational beliefs, 92,
    178, 179, 189–90

G

Gallup research, 76
general manager in
    Roanoke, 63–71, 100,
    109–10
general sales manager in
    Roanoke, 29–30,
    63, 109
Gerstner, Lou, 138–39
get stuff done (GSD) as
    guiding principle,
    132
global culture committee,
    162
goal setting by leaders, 52
God
    asking for support
        from, 155
    confirmation of move
        to Virginia, 30
    guidance from, 4, 144,
        150
    speaking through
        shoeshine guy,
        10
    thanking and
        committing to,
        110
Goldsmith, Marshall, 176
Goleman, Daniel, 66
Good to Great (Collins),
    37, 38, 93, 176–77
Google, 50–51
Google search engine
    placement, 173–74
Grenny, Joseph, 49–50
grow, serve, perform (GSP)
    mentality, 63–83
    Bingham promoted
        to general
        manager, 63–65

and changing beliefs,
    136–37
and emotional
    intelligence,
    66–67
engaging associates,
    76–77
enlightened teams,
    88–89
fitting the person to
    the job, 70–71,
    74, 77–79, 98
hammer/nail
    metaphor, 65–66
introducing at Central
    territory team
    meeting, 160
leader's role in helping
    others, 73–76
Personal Development
    I, 67–71, 85–89,
    92–96, 111–12,
    132
Personal Development
    II, 116
personal-development
    plans, 56, 59–62,
    95–96, 169, 185
purpose as motivator,
    71–72
and systemic approach
    to leadership, 93
and teams, 85–87
tools, 79–83
growth, 73–74
GSP. See grow, serve,
    perform (GSP)
    mentality
guiding principles, 36, 86,
    131–32, 152

H

hammer and nails, 65–66
hiring-process steps, 82–83
hiring tool, 81–83
hospital project for
    mechanical
    engineering
    company, 2–4
hotline for Fix It forum
    ideas, 126–27
humility, 37–38, 148, 163,

164–65, 176–77
Huntsville, Alabama, 17
Huntsville Hospital, 19–20

I

IBM, 138–39
ideas
    from associates,
        109–12
    brainstorming, 94, 96
    employees being heard,
        49–50
    for Fix It forum, 125,
        126–27
    ground up delivery of
        excellence, 113–
        14, 122, 133,
        147, 153–54, 173
    as team property, 27
incentive as motivator, 71
inclusion, trust-based, 21
individual planning, 169
Influencer (Patterson, et.
    al), 49–50
Ingersoll Rand (IR), 152,
    156
integrity, 1–15
    accepting responsibility
        for decisions,
        11–12, 14–15
    of coworkers and
        peers, 12
    and foundational
        beliefs, 179–80
    living with, 5–6
    and profit, 6
    specs for hospital
        project, 2–4
    success from living
        with, 5–6
    tools, 12–15
    trust and, 22–23
    truth and, 7–10
intent and intention
    and building culture,
        86
    and delegation, 26
    and dialogue, 27, 57
    of helping people serve
        their purpose,
        78–79
    and ineptitude, 33

leading with, 74–76
and talent review, 80
and trust, 22
internal motivator, 71–72
interviewing potential new
hires, 82, 83
IR (Ingersoll Rand), 152,
156

J

justifying decisions, 10–11,
14

K

Knapp, Lisa, 158
Krampe, Randy, 160

L

LaCrosse, Wisconsin, 1
ladder of inference, 134,
135, 136–37
leader of dialogue, 27
leaders, 43–62
core behaviors when
dealing with
results, 185–87
and creative tension,
53–54
and culture cards, 162
cutting costs and
driving revenue
chore, 175–76
defining current
culture, 40–41
demeanor of, 148
firing, 150–51
goal setting by, 52
habits leaders must
stop, 176
and hiring process, 83
influence of culture,
37–38, 55
influence on culture,
36, 51, 55
leading versus
directing, 49–50,
55–59, 65–66,
71, 156
leading with intent,
74–76
overview, 31–32
strong leaders, 48, 74,

145, 162–65,
180, 205
tools, 41–42, 55–62
top ten characteristics
lists, 67, 94, 160
and turnover, 50–51
See also coaching;
management;
strong leaders
and culture
leadership
and 360 feedback tool,
55–56, 57–59
Bingham's blunders,
32–34, 71, 147
calibrating leadership
ratings, 80–81
culture team and
core leadership
subjects, 116
discussing in Personal
Development
I, 94
effectiveness related to
strengths and
weaknesses,
163–64
"getting people done
through work,"
70
and hiring process, 83
identifying and
supporting
strengths of
associates, 70–
71, 73–74, 88
Leadership
Competencies
form, 59–62
leadership
development
tool, 165–69
leadership habits tool,
41
leaders' responsibility
for culture
owned by
associates,
147–48
learning and teaching,
vii–viii, 45–46,
100, 182–83
as leverage point, 45–
50, 51–55, 64

Newbern's example,
29, 31–32, 38,
43–44
personal-development
plans, 56, 59–62,
95–96, 169, 185
"speed of trust"
development
program, 154
See also ACBs; entries
starting with
"Personal";
grow, serve,
perform
mentality
Lencioni, Patrick, 168
leverage point, leadership
as, 45–50, 51–55, 64
life's purpose, experiences
fulfilling, viii
listening, 14
Littman, Jonathan, 93
Loyalty Effect, The
(Reichheld), 23

M

Maister, David, 93
management
building-automation
team, 18–20
Central territory vice
president, 143–
47, 153, 155,
156–57, 158,
180–82
employee training
sabotaged by,
49–50
and experiences/beliefs
of associates,
136–37
focusing on financials
versus
customers and
associates, 103
general manager in
Roanoke, 63–71,
100, 109–10
general sales manager
in Roanoke,
29–30, 63, 109
strategy and marketing
for Trane North

America, 129–33
Virginia district manager in Richmond, 110–11, 119–20
See also leaders
Martin, Diane, 112, 114–16
Martin, Mike, 111–12
Maslow, Abraham, 75–76
Maxfield, David, 49–50
Maxwell, John, 167
McMillan, Ron, 49–50
mechanical engineering company, 2–4
metrics for business reviews, 103
Milestones, Fit It, 123
Mill Mountain Theatre, 177–78
mission, 36, 86, 131
mistakes
benefits from, 147–48
cost of, 2
making changes during second week at Roanoke, 32–33
managing long-term results as, 176
as part of being human, 147, 163
motivation, 71–72

N
nails and hammer, 65–66
Newbern, Jess, 29, 31–32, 38, 43–44

O
On Dialogue (Bohm), 27
"one big dinghy" as guiding principle, 132
one-time events, 106
open-forum strategy, 94

P
Patterson, Kerry, 49–50
PDPs (personal-development plans), 56, 59–62, 96, 169, 185
people-building class, 168.

See also skills; talents
people skill development, 69
People Styles at Work and Beyond (Bolton and Bolton), 95
perfection versus excellence, 52
performance
bringing products to market more quickly, 121
fitting the person to the job, 70–71, 74, 77–79
high standard on, 51
leaders' responsibility to help associates, 73–74
levers driving, 46–49, 53
performance-improvement plan, 78–79, 80, 148
performance-management planning process, 169
See also ACBs; profit
Personal Development I, 67–71, 85–89, 92, 111–12, 132
Personal Development II, 116
personal-development plans (PDPs), 56, 59–62, 96, 169, 185
personal growth, 68, 96
Pink, Daniel, 23, 71
politics of a bad culture, 38–40
Practice What You Preach (Maister), 93
pricing and demand, 175
problem solving versus hair pulling, 19–20
proficiency scale, 59–62
profit
Central territory, 158, 180–82
contracting businesses with enlightened teams, 87, 99

and culture, vii, 37, 148–49, 151
and customers, 101–2
from efficient and effective work, 22–23
and GSP mentality, 76–77
from high performance team development, 87
identifying core issues and fixing them, 172–74
integrity and, 6
levers to drive performance, 46, 53
and tenure of associates, 23
and VaWay, 119–20
See also results as the starting point
pro forma of why hiring is important, 82
program managers for Fix It forum, 123, 124–27
purpose as motivator, 71–72

Q
quality and delegation, 25

R
Regnery, David, 145, 158, 161–62
Reichheld, Frederick F., 23
relationship awareness, 86–87, 89
reminders and delegation process, 26
respect
direct with respect, 12–14, 26, 94, 95, 132, 148, 167–68
hammer versus, 65–66
and intention, 74–76
trust versus, 22
responsibility
establishing

expectations,
measurements,
and
accountability,
169
owning a problem, 45
taking responsibility
for decisions,
11–12, 14–15,
113
results as the starting point,
171–87
beginning cultureship,
180–83
as feedback belief, 179
financial results,
174–77
identifying core
problems and
fixing them,
172–74
reinventing, 177–78
and system of beliefs,
178–80
tools, 183–87
See also feedback;
profit
Roanoke City Schools,
Roanoke, Virginia,
39–40, 48–49
Roanoke MS Dinner of
Champions, 53–54

S

Sandys, Celia, 93
Scaccia, Mellisa, 149
schools
areas of focus (levers)
for improving,
46–49
Roanoke City Schools,
39–40, 48–49
student retention
programs, 90–91
search engine placement,
173–74
Seek, Gary, 33
self-assessment/self-rating,
59–62, 67, 94–96,
160
self-awareness, 66–71, 86–
87. See also Personal
Development I

Senge, Peter, 53, 72, 167
service department and
technicians, 64,
172–74
service to others
leaders' responsibility
to help
associates, 73–74
mom's advice, 2
results of Personal
Development
I, 67
shoeshine guy, 9–10
value added to
customers'
businesses, 4–5
Shaver, Eddie, 23–24
"shit" accounts, 1–2
shoeshine service, 9–10
Simon, Dr., 66–67
skills
and delegation, 26
identifying skills
required for jobs
in company,
81–82
improving with group
feedback, 68–70
leaders' responsibility
to associates,
73–76
and personal-
development
plans, 59–62
practicing in a new
arena, 120
top ten leadership
characteristics
lists, 67, 94, 160
unconscious
competency
versus, 65
Smart, Bradford, 81–83,
167
Smith, David, 86–87, 88,
97–98, 99
social styles, 95
Speed of Trust (Covey),
22, 154
"speed of trust"
development
program, 154
standards of excellence, 94,
167–68

strategic actions, 46
strategic processes, 191
strategic training, 191
strategy team leader, Trane
North America,
129–33
strengths, identifying and
supporting, 70–71,
73–74, 88
strong leaders and culture,
143–69
choosing leaders for
teams, 162, 167
overview, 162–65
school principals as, 48
strong leaders follow
culture as
structural belief,
145, 162–65,
180, 205
as structural belief, 180
talking candidly about
individual
results, 74
tools, 165–69
See also ACBs,
enrolling district
leaders in;
changing the
current culture
structural beliefs, 92, 93,
178–79, 180, 190
student retention programs
for schools, 90–91
Swaim, Tammy, 34
Switzler, Al, 49–50
system of beliefs
and changing culture,
134–37
overview, 92, 93,
178–80
putting it all together,
154
See also ACBs;
Cultureship
Plan

T

tactical processes, 191
tactical training, 190–91
talents
awareness at team
level, 160

development of, 168
identifying, 82, 91
talent review tool,
79–81
top ten leadership
characteristics
lists, 67, 94, 160
teams, natural desire to be
great, 137, 158
teamwork
bringing products to
market more
quickly, 121
building automation
team, 18–20
calibrating leadership
ratings, 80–81
core behaviors when
dealing with
results, 185–87
and culture, 35–36, 45
culture team, 115–20
decision making, 44
as focus of IBM
turnaround, 139
great leaders and high
performance, 51
growing team
members, 76
ideas as team property,
27
members' assumptions
about, 137
at Roanoke office,
32–34
teaching district
managers about,
160–61
trusting others and,
20–21
utilizing members, 54
See also enlightened
teams
Thoreau, Henry David, 8
360 feedback tool, 55–56,
57–59
timeliness, 52
timesaving with delegation,
25
tools
100%–0% approach to
life, 11, 14–15,

56–57
360 feedback, 55–56,
57–59
business operating
system, 106–7,
194, 196–201
company systems, 42
culture-development
process, 140–42
cultureship scorecard,
183–87
delegation, 25–26
dialogue, 27
dialogue learning,
166–69
direct with respect,
12–14, 26, 94,
95, 132, 148,
167–68
"Fix It" forum, 118–19,
121–27, 133
hiring, 81–83
leadership habits, 41
overview, 189–91
personal-development
plans, 56, 59–62,
92–96, 95–96,
169, 185
talent review, 79–81
three questions, 55,
56–57
See also feedback
Top Grading (Smart), 167
Topgrading (Smart), 81–83
top ten leadership
characteristics lists,
67, 94, 160
Trane
culture-development
process, 119
efficiency advantage, 3
guiding principles, 152
one culture card for
entire company,
162
Roanoke office, 29
strategy team for Trane
North America,
129–33
training for new sales
engineers, 1
trust, 17–27

of customers, 2–4, 104
delegation tool, 25–26
dialogue tool, 27
in difficult situations,
25
and foundational
beliefs, 179–80
learning the lesson,
17–20, 23–24
mutual distrust versus,
149, 150–51
relationships as
priority, 22–23
respect versus, 22
teamwork as, 20–21
three questions tool,
55, 56–57
tools, 24–27
two-way street of,
20–21
truth and integrity, 7–10
turnover, 23, 50–51, 77, 185

U
ultimate beliefs, 92, 179,
180, 190
underperformers, 80
updates, requesting during
delegation process,
26

V
value added
to customers'
businesses, 4–5
with efficiency
increase, 114
by feedback, 58
reactive actions versus,
175
trusting others for, 21
values, 5, 159
VaWay (The Virginia Way),
117–20
Virginia district Denison
Culture Survey
results, 119
Virginia district manager in
Richmond, 110–11,
119–20

Virginia district manager
    position, 110
Virginia district team, 89,
    99
Virginia Way, The (VaWay),
    117–20
vision
    ACBs, for Central
        territory, 146,
        153, 155
    leading associates to,
        54–55
    overview, 36
    as part of cultural
        clarity, 86, 137
    presenting to others,
        131, 146
voluntary attrition rate, 185

W

Wampler, Lori, 35
Watson, Jeff
    and Bingham, 30, 33–
        34, 66–67, 143
    discussions about
        culture, 44
    as first territory vice
        president, 109
    as great leader, 66–67
    moving to Richmond,
        32
    on strategy and
        marketing
        position for
        Trane North
        America, 129
    talks with, about
        culture, 44
We Shall Not Fail (Sandys
    and Littman), 93
What Got You Here Won't
    Get You There
    (Goldsmith), 176
Wilson, Felix, 109–10, 157
Wolfe, Jeff, 65–66

Z

Zenger, John H., 163–64,
    167

About the Author

Jason Bingham is currently responsible for the $1.2 billion Central territory as vice president for Trane North America. His previous role was as vice president of customer strategy for Trane North America. Before that he was district manager for Trane's Virginia district. Under his leadership and guidance, Trane has created a winning culture globally, nationally, and regionally, which has led to exceeding business expectations every year of his twenty-two-year career. Through his efforts, Trane and the Virginia district have received multiple regional and national awards and distinctions.

Jason has developed strategies, planning processes, and leadership curriculums that have now been distributed across the nation. He holds a bachelor of science in electrical engineering from the University of Tennessee. His involvement in the Roanoke community includes: vice chairman of Roanoke City School Board (six years), executive board member of Mill Mountain Theatre, executive board member of Roanoke Valley Business Council, and chairman of the MS Dinner of Champions.

CPSIA information can be obtained at www.ICGtesting.com
Printed in the USA
LVOW01s1437161013

357226LV00018B/1155/P